KINGDOM WEALTH
The Blueprint for Prosperity

Christopher Turney

© 2025 Christopher Turney
All rights reserved.

No part of this book may be reproduced, stored in a retrieval system, or transmitted in any form or by any means, electronic, mechanical, photocopying, recording, or otherwise, without the prior written permission of the publisher, except for brief quotations used in reviews, articles, or scholarly reference.

ISBN: 979-8-218-80688-0 (paperback)
　　　979-8-218-80745-0 (hardcover)

Printed in the United States of America

For permissions or inquiries, contact:
Chris@krmchurch.com
www.krmchurch.com

Unless otherwise indicated, Scripture quotations are taken from the New King James Version®. Copyright © 1982 by Thomas Nelson. Used by permission. All rights reserved.

Scripture Credits

Some Scripture quotations may also be taken from other translations and are noted accordingly:
- The Amplified Bible (AMP), © 2015 by The Lockman Foundation
- English Standard Version (ESV), © 2001 by Crossway
- New Living Translation (NLT), © 1996, 2004, 2015 by Tyndale House Foundation

Dedication

To Jill, my beloved wife and greatest earthly treasure, thank you for believing in the vision, walking in obedience, and carrying the weight of Kingdom purpose with unwavering grace.

To our children may you be blessed as I endeavor to walk in integrity. *"The man who walks in integrity, blessed are his sons after him"* Proverbs 20:7 (ESV)

To the sons and daughters of the Kingdom,
who refuse to settle for lack or bow to greed,
may you prosper in purpose, walk in wisdom,
and steward what heaven places in your hands.

To every believer who has struggled under the burden of poverty, misunderstood the purpose of prosperity, or been wounded by the extremes, this is for your healing, your clarity, and your freedom.

May you rise in Kingdom wealth and never forget:
You are blessed to be a blessing!

Endorsements

In fifty plus years of ministry I have read many books on the subject of prosperity. Most are formula based, while well-meaning and applicable I have not read one based on true relationship and sonship. Apostle Chris Turney breaks down and reveals what I believe is a truly revelatory book on kingdom provision without all the fear-based teaching in so many I've read. I highly recommend this read. It will help make clear your path to true kingdom prosperity. It will cause us to walk in great freedom developing faith to prosper.

Bishop Gary Clowers
Founder of FWCMI & Family Worship Center Ministries,
Fremont, Ohio

This book is a much-needed revelation on Kingdom wealth. My friend, Apostle Chris Turney, powerfully shows that true Kingdom wealth is not measured in possessions but in the dethroning of self and the enthroning of Jesus Christ. It is a spirit of generosity that reaches beyond earthly treasures into legacy, dynasty, and the continuation of Christ's eternal throne. With both clarity and depth, these pages unveil divine truths of how Kingdom wealth is to be understood and lived out in our daily lives. Whether you are a leader guiding other's, or a believer seeking to walk faithfully with our Lord Jesus Christ, you will find wisdom and revelation here.

This book magnifies God's Kingdom and points us to the true riches that only Jesus can give.

Ambassador Jana Alcorn
Hope Culture
Nashville, Tennessee

God's Kingdom concept of wealth is unfolded in practical understanding by Apostle Chris Turney. He reveals that the treasure in our earthen vessels is not first money, but generosity from a spiritual vault of resources, God placed inside us before we were born. Wealth is from the inside out and is not activated until it's transferred to others through God's eternal purpose. Apostle Chris continues to reveal this Kingdom principle set in intrinsic wealth, that it is deposited and activated in sonship through covenant of inheritance sealed with promise. I wholeheartedly endorse every page of this revelatory book that corrects misunderstanding around the 'prosperity gospel' and reveals the authentic wealth of the Kingdom in you.

Dr. Rick Kendall
Founder of Victory Ministries

Table of Contents

Foreword *1*

Preface *3*

Introduction *5*

1. The Lie of Lack 9
2. God is not Poor 17
3. Provision was in the Garden 23
4. Manna or Multiplication? 29
5. Poverty is a Mindset Before it's a Condition 35
6. The Purpose of Prosperity 43
7. The False Gospel of Greed 49
8. Wealth without Worship is Dangerous 57
9. The Power to get Wealth 65
10. Grace-giving, the Prosperity of Sons 73
11. Stewardship, Managing what Heaven Trusts you With 79
12. Sowing and Reaping in the Kingdom 87
13. Contentment and Increase, Friends, not Enemies 95
14. Kingdom Economics, Heaven's System in the Earth 101
15. Legacy Wealth, Leaving an Inheritance of Vision and Value 111
16. The Inheritance of Sons: Wealth as a Birthright 117
17. Generational Wealth and Kingdom Legacy 121
18. The Currency of Honor 125
19. The Wealth of Nations 129
20. Kingdom Wealth and Apostolic Assignment 133
21. The Inheritance of Sons and Daughters 137

About the Author *143*

Foreword

The first time my wife and I heard Chris Turney, minister, it was at a meeting a friend had recommended we attend. As we listened to Chris speak. Something stirred in our spirits. He was teaching things that challenged our entrenched religious thinking and beliefs. But there a was a peace, that said this is solid biblical Kingdom teaching. We realized this was a man that loved the Lord and had the courage to share the truth of the Kingdom, even if it meant swimming against the current in the river of religion. This started a relationship with Apostle Chris and a pursuit of the Kingdom that has lasted over 30 years.

I have been in the financial services industry for over 25 years. My interaction with clients includes tax reduction, asset protection, investment management and legacy planning.

So, when Apostle Chris asked me to write the foreword for this book, **Kingdom Wealth**, I enthusiastically agreed. When I read in the introduction; *"In the Kingdom, prosperity has a purpose, wealth has a mission, and increase is connected to assignment, not indulgence."* I was hooked and couldn't put the book down until I had finished it.

Kingdom Wealth did exactually what the subtitle says. It gave me a biblical blueprint for prosperity.

Over all my years in the financial industry, I have read many books, taken many classes and listened to countless podcasts and webinars. But this book by Apostle Chris has explained with ringing clarity the foundation for accumulating and managing wealth.

When I finished the book, there was excitement and confidence for a proven strategy that could be shared with both individuals and business clients. No matter what was happening on the world stage; market fluctuations or in the financial culture, it wouldn't fail. As Apostle Chris writes, *"Kingdom offers a foundation that cannot be shaken."*

Kingdom Wealth is written so that it could be used for small groups, or a classroom setting. Whether you are a pastor, business owner or individual, this book will give you foundational material to teach, apply to your business, and live by.

Apostle Chris thank you for writing this book. It will certainly fill a void!

Mark Ellington
Partner in DR Financial Group and ProTax LP
Wealth Management

Preface

There's a sound rising in the Body of Christ, a call to come out of the caves of survival and step into the light of Kingdom abundance. For too long, the conversation around money has either been poisoned by greed or silenced by guilt. And in both cases, the result has been the same: stagnation, shame, and stunted purpose.

This book was birthed from a burden, not to enter a debate, but to deliver clarity. I've watched good-hearted believers struggle under the weight of religious poverty mindsets, falsely believing that lack was somehow godly. I've also watched others chase after "prosperity" that was nothing more than self-promotion dressed in spiritual language.

But I believe there's a remnant rising. A remnant who refuses to be poor, but also refuses to be proud. A remnant who won't be seduced by the idolatry of wealth, but also won't apologize for walking in provision. A remnant who understands that the Kingdom is not broke, and neither should they be.

This is not a prosperity manual. It's a Kingdom manifesto. A declaration that God does provide, but not for our ego, He provides for His purposes.

As you read these pages, I pray two things happen:

1. Strongholds of lack break off your mind, and you begin to see prosperity as part of your inheritance, not a forbidden indulgence.

2. False ideas of extravagant greed are exposed, and you return to the pure joy of stewarding Kingdom resources with integrity.

Whether you're a pastor, a business leader, a parent, or a pioneer, this book is for you. It's time to reject both poverty and pride and walk the narrow road of prosperity with purpose.

Welcome to the revelation of Kingdom Wealth.

Christopher Turney

Introduction

Breaking silence on money and breaking the cycle of lack, without breaking trust in the Word.

Money has long been a controversial subject in the Church. For some, it's a taboo topic to avoid; for others, it has become a manipulative tool. On one side, people have embraced poverty as a form of piety, wearing lack like a badge of humility. On the other, prosperity preaching has sometimes devolved into excessive, manipulative fundraising, sowing seeds not of faith, but of pressure.

I wrote this book because we desperately need a Kingdom correction. Not a reaction. Not a pendulum swing. A revelation.

It's time to break the poverty mindset, the one that whispers, "You're unworthy to prosper." The one that reduces provision to mere survival. The one that spiritualizes lack as though God takes pleasure in seeing His children struggle. That's not the God of the Bible.

But it's also time to expose the extreme prosperity gospel that turns Jesus into a lottery ticket and equates abundance with worth. Extravagance does not equal anointing. And gain is not always godliness.

The truth is found in the Kingdom.

In the Kingdom, prosperity has a purpose. Wealth has a mission. And increase is connected to assignment, not indulgence.

When God placed Adam in the garden, He placed him in a finished work, a land with soil, seed, and a river. There was no need for

Adam to strive or toil to survive. He was positioned to steward abundance and produce fruit. That picture of Kingdom provision is still true today. God doesn't want you just getting by, He wants you living in the overflow of His purpose.

But let me be clear: Kingdom wealth is not a status symbol, it's a stewardship responsibility. You are not blessed to flaunt. You are blessed to build. You are not favored to consume. You are favored to fulfill Kingdom assignment.

This book is for:
- The one tired of religious guilt around money
- The one disillusioned by manipulative giving schemes
- The one ready to prosper with integrity and purpose
- The one who knows there's more, but doesn't want to compromise

Throughout these chapters, we'll break down the lie of lack, uproot the orphan spirit behind hoarding and striving, confront the false prosperity gospel, and recover the truth of God's design for Kingdom abundance.

We'll explore Eden, Israel, Jesus' teachings, Paul's letters, and the pattern of provision throughout Scripture, not just as theory but as a framework for living.

God is raising up a people who will prosper with purpose, who will not bow to Mammon, but who also refuse to live beneath their inheritance.

This isn't about opulence. It's about obedience. It's not about riches for self, it's about resources for Kingdom purpose.

Let's recover the original blueprint.

KINGDOM WEALTH

Let's break the mindset of barely enough.
Let's build lives that reflect Heaven's economy.
Let's walk in Kingdom Wealth.

Chapter 1
The Lie of Lack

"The Lord is my shepherd; I shall not want." Psalm 23:1 (NKJV)

The Lie That Masquerades as Humility
Some lies sound noble.
Some lies quote Scripture.
Some lies even wear the mask of humility.

One of the most damaging lies ever introduced to the people of God is the idea that lack is somehow holy, that poverty equals purity, and that struggling financially is a sign of spiritual maturity.

It's a lie.

A dangerous, disempowering lie that has kept generations of believers stuck, silent, and starving in areas where they were meant to reign.

The enemy doesn't mind you worshipping as long as you're broke. He doesn't mind your passion as long as you're powerless. And the quickest way to keep people powerless is to convince them that prosperity is ungodly.

But the first words out of God's mouth toward mankind were not about deprivation, they were about dominion and blessing (Genesis 1:28). From the very beginning, God set humanity in an environment of abundance, not to consume, but to steward. Lack wasn't holy; it was unthinkable.

And interestingly, the first blessing spoken over any creature was upon the fish (Genesis 1:22). Then, in Genesis 1:28, when God gave mankind dominion, the first area He assigned was "over the fish of the sea." This was no coincidence.

Throughout Scripture, the fish becomes a consistent sign of God's provision and purpose:
- It was a great fish that carried Jonah back into alignment with his assignment.
- It was a coin in the mouth of a fish that paid Jesus' temple tax, divine provision through unexpected means.
- It was a miraculous catch of fish that marked the calling of the disciples.
- It was Jesus who said, "Cast your net on the other side," and suddenly there was overflow where moments before there had been nothing.

The fish points to a truth we must not miss: God's economy doesn't operate by effort alone; it responds to obedience and assignment. Where God gives dominion, He also appoints supply. The fish of the sea are not just symbols of natural resources, they are prophetic indicators that when we move in alignment with God's word, even the hidden things of the deep will respond.

Lack was never part of the design.
- Dominion was.
- Abundance was.

And provision flows through revelation and obedience.

The Garden Was Full
God didn't place Adam in a wilderness, He placed him in a garden.

Not just any garden, but Eden. A name that means delight, abundance, pleasure.

Genesis 2 describes Eden as a place with:
- Trees that were pleasant to the sight and good for food
- Rivers that nourished the land
- Gold, bdellium, and onyx stone
- A finished work, lacking nothing

Adam never had to ask for provision, he was placed in it. He was not created in poverty and asked to believe for wealth. He was created in wealth and asked to tend it.

Provision preceded purpose.
Supply was there before the assignment.

The lie of lack says you must strive for what God has already provided. It whispers that struggle is your portion and that contentment means settling for less. But the truth of Kingdom wealth is this: God starts with more than enough.

Lack Entered Through Sin, Not Design

Lack was not part of creation, it was the consequence of the Fall.

It wasn't until sin entered that scarcity appeared:

> *"Cursed is the ground for your sake.*
> *In toil you shall eat of it…*
> *Both thorns and thistles it shall bring forth for you."*
> (Genesis 3:17–18)

Adam went from tending abundance to surviving through toil.
From freely receiving to painfully producing.

Lack didn't come from God's design; it came from man's disconnection.

To believe that God desires you to live in lack is to believe that the consequences of sin are the will of God. But Jesus didn't come to leave you in that condition. He came to redeem you from the curse, including the curse of scarcity.

Jesus Broke the Back of Lack
Everywhere Jesus went, lack lost its power.

He turned water into wine.
He fed multitudes with a few loaves and fishes.
He pulled coins from a fish's mouth.
He filled empty nets until they nearly broke.
He made nothing into something, over and over again.

Why?
Because He was showing us the nature of the Kingdom.

Jesus did not teach His disciples to tolerate lack.
He taught them how to multiply.
He sent them out with authority, and when they returned, He asked:

> *"When I sent you without money bag, knapsack, and sandals, did you lack anything?"* So they said, *"Nothing."* (Luke 22:35, NKJV)

Even in their lack of supply, there was no lack of provision.

He wasn't teaching them to be poor. He was teaching them to trust.

Scarcity Is a Mindset
You can have money and still live in lack.
You can have resources and still think like a beggar.

KINGDOM WEALTH

You can drive a nice car and still fear losing it all.

Why?

Because lack is a mindset before it's a condition
It starts in the soul. And the only thing that can deliver you from it is truth.

The poverty mindset says:
- "There's never enough."
- "I shouldn't want more."
- "If I succeed, I'm no longer humble."
- "Money is evil."
- "I feel guilty for being blessed."

But the Word says:
- *"The Lord is my shepherd, I shall not want."* (Psalm 23:1)
- *"The young lions lack and suffer hunger; but those who seek the Lord shall not lack any good thing."* (Psalm 34:10)
- *"My God shall supply all your need according to His riches in glory."* (Philippians 4:19)

Why the Enemy Loves This Lie
When believers believe the lie of lack:
- The Kingdom stalls because generosity dries up
- The gospel suffers because resources are withheld
- The Church shrinks back from vision because of fear of funding

Satan doesn't need to make you evil. He just needs to make you empty.

But we weren't made for lack.
We were made for abundant life (John 10:10).

And abundance doesn't start with income, it starts with understanding.

Breaking the Lie

You don't have to chase riches to break lack.
You don't have to deny your blessings to stay holy.

What you do need is a renewed mind, one that sees money not as a master or a measure of worth, but as a means for Kingdom impact.

Jesus didn't say, *"Blessed are the poor"* He said, *"Blessed are the poor in spirit."* (Matthew 5:3)

The **poor in spirit** are those that remain dependent on God, which is a show of faith. It is not saying that we are blessed if we resign to living in poverty, which is believing a lie. The one is faith. The other is a lie.

Declaration
I was not created for lack.
I was placed in a finished work.
I reject the lie that poverty is holy.
I receive Kingdom provision as my birthright.
I am blessed to be a blessing.

Reflection Questions
1. How does Genesis 1:28 reshape your view of God's intent for provision?
2. In what ways have you embraced or resisted the idea of dominion as connected to prosperity?
3. What areas of your life reflect abundance? What areas reflect lack, and why?
4. How do you view stewardship as part of divine blessing?

"You are not poor because you lack money. You are poor when you lack access to Kingdom truth."

Dr. Myles Munroe

Chapter 2
God is not Poor

The Nature of the Provider
"The earth is the Lord's, and all its fullness, The world and those who dwell therein."   Psalm 24:1 (NKJV)

Rethinking the Source
Let's start with a foundational truth:
God is not poor.
He never has been. He never will be.

Poverty is not part of His nature. Scarcity is not in His vocabulary. And heaven is not on a budget.

Yet many believers live with an unspoken assumption that God is reluctant to provide, stingy with His blessing, or passive toward their need. This is not theology, it's trauma disguised as humility. And it's time to confront it.

If you believe God is withholding from you, you will either beg Him for what is already yours, or worse, you'll settle for far less than what He's freely given. But the problem is not in the heavens, it's in the mindset.

To walk in Kingdom wealth, you must know this:
The nature of the Provider determines the flow of provision.

Abundance Is Who He Is
Provision is not something God occasionally does, it's who He perpetually is.

From the beginning, He revealed Himself by name:
- Jehovah-Jireh – The Lord Will Provide (Genesis 22:14)
- El Shaddai – The All-Sufficient One (Genesis 17:1)
- The God of More Than Enough – (2 Corinthians 9:8 paraphrased)

When God provided a ram for Abraham, it wasn't a one-time miracle. It was a revelation of His nature. God was saying, "This is who I am, I see the need before you do, and I meet it before you get there."

The truth is: God does not become provision in response to your need. He already is provision.
He is I AM, not I might be or I hope to be.

Creation Was Extravagant

God's first act toward humanity was not salvation, it was creation. And when He created, He did not skimp. He didn't give Adam just enough oxygen to breathe or a minimal plot of dry ground.

He gave:
- Rivers with four branches
- Trees both beautiful and edible
- Gold, bdellium, and onyx stone
- A garden of delight with unbroken fellowship

Why? Because God is not utilitarian, He's a Father. And Fathers prepare before the child ever arrives.

This is a divine pattern: God finishes the environment before He places the person. He doesn't put man in a work-in-progress. He places man in a finished work. The same is true today. You were born into a plan already established, and provision is already in the assignment.

Jesus Never Modeled Scarcity

Jesus, the exact image of the Father, never modeled lack. He was born into simplicity, yes, but not poverty. And even in the absence of visible resources, He always operated in overflow.

When there wasn't enough, He blessed and broke what was there, and it multiplied.

When there was no money for taxes, He didn't take up an offering, He spoke to the fish.

When the wine ran out, He didn't panic, He transformed the water.

Jesus didn't just teach about the Father's provision, He demonstrated it. He didn't glorify poverty. He glorified the Provider.

Provision Is Personal

God's provision is not mechanical, it's relational.

He's not your vending machine, He's your Father.

Jesus said, *"Your Father knows what you need before you ask Him"* (Matthew 6:8)

And again: *"If you then, being evil, know how to give good gifts to your children, how much more will your Father in heaven give...?"* (Luke 11:13)

This is the core issue: Your view of God determines your posture in provision.

If you see Him as reluctant, you'll beg.
If you see Him as indifferent, you'll strive.
If you see Him as El Shaddai, you'll trust.
If you see Him as Father, you'll rest.

Kingdom wealth begins not with money in your hand, but with the right image of God in your heart.

Poverty Offends His Nature
Let's be blunt:
To glorify poverty as if it pleases God is to misrepresent His heart.

While Scripture does speak of the poor being blessed, it never equates poverty with divine approval. Jesus became poor that we through His poverty might be made rich (2 Corinthians 8:9). This richness isn't just spiritual. It includes sufficiency, abundance, and ability to supply every good work (2 Corinthians 9:8).

God is not impressed by scarcity, and He's not honored by struggle for struggle's sake.

Poverty offends His nature because it robs His children of dignity, mobility, and generosity.

The Provider Has a Purpose
God's nature is provision, but His purpose is assignment.

He provides to:
- Fund His purposes
- Advance His Kingdom
- Bless His people
- Demonstrate His goodness to the world

He doesn't make you a reservoir, He makes you a river. And rivers flow. They don't hoard. They give life everywhere they go.

Declaration
My God is not poor.

He is not reluctant. He is not indifferent.
He is Jehovah-Jireh, my Provider and my Father.
I reject the image of a stingy God.
I embrace the truth: abundance is in His nature, and provision is in His plan.

Reflection Questions
1. What limiting beliefs about money or provision have you inherited or internalized?
2. How has fear of lack shaped your decisions?
3. Where have you seen poverty mindset disguised as false humility?
4. What does it look like to think as a Kingdom son instead of a spiritual orphan?

Chapter 3
Provision was in the Garden

> *"Then the Lord God took the man and put him in the garden of Eden to tend and keep it."*   Genesis 2:15 (NKJV)

Provision Preceded Purpose

Before man was ever told to work, build, or tend, God had already provided everything he would need. Adam was not created and then told to survive. He was created and placed into a finished work.

This is not just a historical detail; it is a Kingdom principle.

God did not wait for man to pray before He made trees for food, rivers for water, or gold in the ground. He completed the environment before He placed the person.

Why? Because God is a Father, and fathers prepare. He doesn't call you into something without first equipping it with what you'll need.

If you're still wondering if God will provide for your purpose, you're asking the wrong question. The real question is: Are you in the place He set you? Because where He places you, He also plants provision.

The Garden Had Everything, In Seed Form

Genesis 2 reveals that Eden wasn't just a lush paradise, it was a **loaded provision center**. It had:
- Every tree that was pleasant to the eyes and good for food
- A river that flowed and parted into four heads
- Gold, bdellium, and onyx stone

- Atmosphere, soil, seed, and assignment

Everything Adam needed was present, but not everything was obvious.

Much of what God provided was still in seed form. That's the **mystery of Kingdom wealth**: God doesn't always give you fruit, He gives you seed.

He gives:
- Soil to plant in
- Seed to sow
- Water to flow
- And an assignment to cultivate

If you don't understand this, you'll miss the provision because you were looking for something finished instead of something hidden.

The River Was the Life Source

Genesis 2:10 says, *"Now a river went out of Eden to water the garden, and from there it parted and became four riverheads."*

This is a divine picture: God placed a flow in the center of provision.

The river didn't just make the garden lush, it distributed life.

The names of the four rivers, Pishon, Gihon, Hiddekel (Tigris), and Euphrates, each carry prophetic meaning. They represent:
- Increase (Pishon)
- Bursting forth (Gihon)
- Rapid/Swift (Hiddekel)
- Fruitfulness (Euphrates)

These are not just poetic details. They are spiritual codes. God's provision flows where there is increase, movement, acceleration, and fruitfulness. Wherever the river flows, life happens.

So here's the question: Are you planted near the river?

The Psalmist said,
> "He shall be like a tree planted by the rivers of water, That brings forth its fruit in its season… and whatever he does shall prosper."
> (Psalm 1:3)

Your prosperity is connected to your proximity to the flow.

You Were Placed, Not Randomly Positioned
Genesis 2:15 says God took the man and placed him in the garden.

That word "placed" in Hebrew (נוח, nuach) means to rest, to set down securely, to settle into. Adam wasn't dropped into Eden as a visitor, he was positioned there by divine intent.

Where God places you, He provides for you.
Where God plants you, He waters you.

This truth is vital for those chasing provision outside of purpose. Don't run to a new field if the problem isn't the ground, it's the fact that you've stopped tending it.

God's provision is often locked in the place of your assignment. If you've been set somewhere, whether it's a church, a city, a business, or a team, stop looking for greener grass and start discovering the gold in the ground.

Tending Unlocks the Increase
God didn't give Adam a finished plate of fruit.
He gave him a garden to tend and keep.

That word "tend" (עָבַד, avad) means to work, cultivate, or serve. "Keep" (שָׁמַר, shamar) means to guard, protect, or steward.

In other words, provision wasn't **passive**. It was **participatory**.

God provided the raw materials, Adam brought stewardship. The increase was already there, but it was unlocked through responsibility.

This is where many miss Kingdom wealth. They expect increase with no cultivation. But abundance doesn't come to the lazy, it comes to the faithful.

Eden Is a Pattern, Not Just a Paradise

Don't miss this: Eden is not just a distant memory of paradise, it's a pattern for how God still operates.

He places His sons in finished works.
He supplies the seed, the soil, and the stream.
He commissions them to tend and keep.
And He expects fruit, not for food only, but for generational legacy.

Jesus came to restore what Adam lost. Not just heaven, but the Kingdom. And with that restoration comes the recovery of provision, purpose, and placement.

You were never meant to survive outside the garden. You were always meant to walk in provision, tend your ground, and multiply.

Declaration
I am not searching for provision; it's already placed where God set me.
The garden is finished. The seed is in my hand. The river is flowing.

KINGDOM WEALTH

I am not a wanderer; I am a worker in a planted place.
I receive the Eden pattern of Kingdom provision in my life.
I will tend. I will keep. I will multiply.

Reflection Questions
1. Do you trust God as Provider, or do you see Him primarily as Judge or Rescuer?
2. How does creation reflect God's abundance?
3. What are some examples of God providing before there was a need?
4. How can you reflect the Provider-nature of God in your own life?

Chapter 4
Manna or Multiplication?

> *"And you shall remember that the Lord your God led you all the way these forty years... to humble you and test you... so He might make you know that man shall not live by bread alone... but by every word that proceeds from the mouth of the Lord."*
>
> Deuteronomy 8:2–3 (NKJV)

From Miraculous to Managerial

There's a major shift that happens in the life of every believer who walks in Kingdom maturity.

It's the shift from miraculous mercy to managerial multiplication. From daily dependence on falling bread... to producing fruit from planted seed.

When Israel came out of Egypt, God gave them manna from heaven, supernatural bread that showed up every morning. They didn't work for it, grow it, or understand it. In fact, the word manna literally means, "What is it?"

It was a mystery meal that met their immediate need.

But here's the key: manna was never meant to last forever. It was a provision of transition, not a pattern for permanence.

Manna: Provision for the Wilderness, Not the Promise

For forty years, Israel was fed by God's mercy. He gave them what they couldn't provide for themselves. He covered their weakness. He nurtured their immaturity. He sustained their journey.

But when they crossed into the Promised Land, something profound happened:

> *"Then the manna ceased on the day after they had eaten the produce of the land... and the children of Israel no longer had manna, but they ate the food of the land of Canaan that year."*
> (Joshua 5:12, NKJV)

Did you catch that?
The manna stopped.

Not because God stopped being good.
Not because the people sinned.
But because they had entered maturity and inheritance.

God was saying:
"You're not wanderers anymore.
You're possessors now.
The days of bread falling are over, now, you plant, reap, and multiply."

Manna Requires No Stewardship, Just Survival
Manna is mercy, but it doesn't mature you.
It trains you to gather, but not to grow.
It keeps you alive but doesn't advance you.

In the wilderness, God gave daily bread.
In the promise, God gave land, seed, and dominion.

This is critical:
Manna didn't make Israel lazy, it kept them dependent. But not on God's voice, on God's hand. They learned to gather what fell instead of cultivating what was planted.

And this is the trap many believers fall into today. They live from miracle to miracle… crisis to crisis… breakthrough to breakthrough. But the Kingdom was never designed to be lived in perpetual desperation.

You weren't called to beg God for daily bread. You were called to walk in wisdom, plant with purpose, and multiply what He's already placed in your hands.

Multiplication Requires Maturity
The Promised Land is not for the immature.
It requires work, wisdom, and stewardship.

In Egypt, they were slaves.
In the wilderness, they were wanderers.
But in Canaan, they were possessors.

And possessors must know the land, sow the seed, and gather the harvest.

This is where many people pray for prosperity but reject responsibility. They want God to drop provision from the sky, but don't want to develop the skills, strategy, or systems required to sustain increase.

But God does not reward begging, He rewards faithfulness. He gives seed to the sower, not just bread to the hungry (2 Corinthians 9:10).

Multiplication is messy. It takes time. It requires **partnership** with God, not just **petitions** to God.

When Manna Stops, Don't Panic
Many believers freak out when the "easy" provision dries up. Suddenly, the job ends, the miracle doesn't come in the same way, the breakthrough seems delayed.

But this may be a sign, not of divine rejection, but of divine promotion.

God is saying, *"It's time to grow up.*
It's time to sow. It's time to possess this land."

The ceasing of manna is the signal for maturity. It means God now trusts you with more than just enough. He trusts you with the ability to multiply.

The Test of Transition

Deuteronomy 8 reveals that God tested Israel in the wilderness not to crush them, but to teach them. He humbled them with manna so they would understand that life is not found in provision, but in the Word of God.

> *"He fed you with manna... that He might humble you... that He might test you, to do you good in the end."* (Deuteronomy 8:16)

Manna was a means to an end, not the end itself.

And many people settle in the season of manna, thinking it's the height of God's goodness. But God is after something far greater: possession, authority, and overflow.

He wants you to stop asking for daily drops and start walking in divine dominion.

Manna Mindset vs. Multiplication Mindset

Manna Mindset	Multiplication Mindset
Waits for provision to fall	Works the land and sows seed
Asks daily	Plans generationally
Consumes only	Produces and shares
Depends on handouts	Operates in stewardship
Survives	Builds and multiplies

God Wants to Trust You With Seed

Just as Eden was filled with seed-bearing plants, the Promised Land was full of potential. God didn't give Israel a fully developed city, He gave them land to possess.

That means tilling the soil.
Sowing the seed.
Waiting for rain.
And harvesting in due season.

It's slower than manna.
But it's sustainable.
It's generational.
It's Kingdom.

Declaration
I'm not living for manna; I'm walking in multiplication.
I am not dependent on crisis; I'm empowered by covenant.
I will sow, I will tend, I will reap.
My God is not just a God of mercy, He is the God of multiplication.

Reflection Questions
1. Are you living in a manna season or a multiplication season?
2. How has God challenged you to shift from dependence to dominion?
3. What does multiplication require that manna does not?
4. Where do you need to move from survival into strategy?

Chapter 5
Poverty is a Mindset Before it's a Condition

"Beloved, I pray that you may prosper in all things and be in health, just as your soul prospers."   3 John 1:2 (NKJV)

Not Just a Wallet Problem, A Soul Problem
Poverty is not just the absence of money.
It's the absence of a prosperous mindset.

You can put $10,000 in a person's hand, and if they still think poor, they'll lose it. You can upgrade someone's job, but if their identity is rooted in lack, they'll sabotage it. Because poverty doesn't start in the bank, it starts in the belief system.

That's why Scripture doesn't just talk about financial prosperity; it begins with soul prosperity:

"...just as your soul prospers."

The condition of your mind, emotions, and will, your soul, sets the ceiling for what you can sustain. You will never live above the level of your mindset.

The Fruit of a Poverty Mindset
A poverty mindset can wear different clothes. It can sound spiritual. It can look generous. But its fruit is always the same:
- Fear of not having enough
- Shame when blessed
- Suspicion toward wealth
- Inability to receive freely

- Chronic survival mode
- Settling for less than you're called to

This mindset makes you feel guilty for dreaming big. It teaches you to downplay success, so others aren't uncomfortable. It convinces you that to be truly spiritual, you must struggle.

But God's Kingdom is not built on shame, fear, or guilt. It is built on sonship. And sons don't beg for scraps, they walk in access and inheritance.

Poverty Thinking Often Masquerades as Humility

There is a false humility that has crept into the Church, one that confuses lack with meekness and poverty with piety.

It says:
- "I don't need much, I'm content."
- *"I'd rather be poor and holy than rich and carnal."*
- *"I'm just a servant. I don't deserve more."*

But Jesus didn't die to give us small thinking.
He died to restore identity, and identity determines access.

You can be content and still expand.
You can be grateful and still go after more.
True humility is not denying what God gave you, it's stewarding it with honor.

The Israelites Had Egypt in Their Minds

Even after they left Egypt, the Israelites still thought like slaves. They had been delivered externally, but they were still bound internally.

They longed to go back to slavery because they were more familiar with predictable lack than with uncertain freedom.

God got them out of Egypt in one night.
But it took 40 years to get Egypt out of them.

This is the same struggle many believers face. They've been saved, but they haven't been renewed. They've left the land of bondage, but bondage hasn't left their thinking.

Jesus Came to Heal the Broken and Poor in Spirit
In Luke 4, Jesus declared His mission:

> "The Spirit of the Lord is upon Me... to preach the gospel to the poor..."

This was not a message limited to those without money. The word poor here (Greek: ptōchos) means reduced to begging, lacking identity, void of worth.

He came to bring good news to those who had believed the lie of lack, those who had been crushed by systems, shamed by religion, or trapped by generational poverty.

The gospel restores dignity, identity, and purpose. It heals the broken-hearted and renews the mindset.

How the Mindset Works: The Orphan vs. the Son
Poverty in the soul is often the fruit of an orphan spirit.
The orphan believes:
- "I have to fight for what's mine."
- "No one is coming to help me."
- "I don't belong at the table."
- "God blesses others, not me."

But a son thinks differently:
- *"Provision is my Father's responsibility."*
- *"I am positioned for inheritance."*
- *"I don't compete, I receive."*
- *"There is more than enough in my Father's house."*

To break poverty thinking, you must shift from orphanhood to sonship. From fear to faith. From survival to stewardship. From self-preservation to Kingdom participation.

Poverty Thinking Fears Increase

Many people reject prosperity because they are afraid of what comes with it.

They fear:
- Becoming prideful
- Being misunderstood
- Having to manage more
- Becoming a target
- Losing what they gain

But all of this is rooted in a scarcity mentality.
It sees increase as a burden instead of a blessing.
It sees wealth as a threat instead of a tool.

Poverty also manifests in the fear of not having enough. Whether a person has little or much, this fear drives them to **cling tightly to what they have,** hesitant to give or share. Generosity becomes threatening, not liberating, because at the root is a belief that *"If I let this go, I might not get it back."*

This is why even people with money can still have a poverty mindset. The issue is not the amount in your account, it's the fear in your heart.

Poverty says: *"If I give, I'll lose."*
Kingdom says: *"If I give, I grow."*

Yet when your mind is renewed by the Kingdom, you stop fearing wealth, you start governing it. You understand that you are not owned by what you possess, you steward it for His glory.

Your Mind Must Prosper Before Your Life Will
Romans 12:2 says:

> *"Be transformed by the renewing of your mind..."*

Your life will not rise above your thinking. If your soul is stuck in lack, your life will reflect it, no matter how many breakthroughs you chase.

This is why some people go from miracle to miracle but never build momentum. They haven't changed their mind, so they keep repeating the same patterns.

God will bless you, but if your thinking is still impoverished, you'll lose what He gives. Prosperity without preparation becomes pressure.

But when your mind is renewed, you no longer fear blessing, you expect it.

You don't worship money, you wield it.
You don't hoard, you flow.

Declaration
I reject every lie that ties my identity to lack.
I am not an orphan; I am a son.

CHRISTOPHER TURNEY

I was made to prosper, inside and out.
My soul is healthy, and my mind is being renewed.
I don't fear blessing, I walk in it with wisdom.
I am breaking every poverty pattern and
stepping into Kingdom abundance.

Reflection Questions
1. How has fear of not having enough affected your generosity?
2. In what ways does Mammon seek to master you?
3. What systems or attitudes in your life might be under Mammon's influence?
4. What would surrendering fully to God's economic system look like for you?

"God prospers me not to raise my standard of living, but to raise my standard of giving."

Randy Alcorn

Chapter 6
The Purpose of Prosperity

Wealth Is for Assignment, Not Amusement
> *"Remember the Lord your God, for it is He who gives you power to get wealth, that He may establish His covenant."*
>   Deuteronomy 8:18 (NKJV)

Prosperity Is Not the Goal, It's the Tool
One of the greatest deceptions surrounding prosperity is that it's about us, our comfort, our status, our pleasure.

But in the Kingdom, wealth is never the goal. It's the tool. It's not the finish line, it's the equipment to run your race.

God gives wealth with an assignment in mind. It's not about getting more stuff; it's about advancing more purpose.

The moment prosperity becomes about amusement, personal luxury, or proving your success, it detaches from Kingdom purpose and slides into self-glorification.

But when wealth is seen as provision for vision, everything changes.

Deuteronomy 8:18: The Key Verse for Kingdom Wealth
> *"It is He who gives you power to get wealth, that He may establish His covenant..."*

This verse dismantles two lies:
1. That God doesn't want you wealthy.
2. That wealth is just for you.

43

It says God gives power to get wealth, not just to meet your needs, but to **establish His covenant**.
In other words: Wealth follows the Word.
Where there is covenant, there is supply.

God funds what He fathers.
He provides for what He plants.
And He gives power (strategy, ideas, strength, opportunity) to get wealth so that His Kingdom can be seen, known, and sustained on the earth.

The Pattern of Purpose-Driven Provision
Throughout Scripture, God gave resources for reasons:
- Joseph was raised up to manage Egypt's wealth, not for status, but to preserve nations (Genesis 41).
- David amassed wealth not to build himself a palace, but to prepare for the temple of the Lord.
- Solomon was given wisdom and wealth, not for amusement, but to rule with justice and reveal God's glory to the nations.
- The women who followed Jesus (Luke 8:1–3) supported His ministry financially, using their resources for divine mission.
- The early Church shared what they had so that "none among them lacked" (Acts 4:34), a community of generous believers who funded Kingdom impact.

In every case, prosperity was a by-product of alignment with assignment. When God prospers you, it's because there's purpose attached to your increase.

What Happens When You Prosper Without Purpose?

- You begin to build your name instead of His.
- You grow greedy or self-indulgent.
- You mistake comfort for calling.

- You believe you earned it, rather than being entrusted with it.

Prosperity without assignment is dangerous.
It leads to pride, disconnection, and self-sufficiency.

This is why many people fall into the trap of using "blessing" language to mask materialism.

They say, "God blessed me," but the blessing is serving their lifestyle instead of His Lordship.

What's the Assignment Behind Your Abundance?
If God blesses you financially, the first question you should ask isn't:
- *"What can I buy?"*

But rather:
- *"What is this for?"*
- *"Who is this for?"*
- *"What vision is this meant to fuel?"*

Maybe the increase is meant to:
- Launch a ministry
- Support missions
- Start a business that funds the Kingdom
- Pay off someone else's debt
- Create generational wealth for your children's children
- Fund a local church's building campaign
- Break cycles of economic oppression in your region

You are not blessed to flaunt.
You are blessed to build.

Extravagance vs. Excellence
Kingdom prosperity doesn't promote extravagance. It promotes **excellence**.

There's a difference.
- Excellence builds quality and stewards well.
- Extravagance chases attention and indulges excess.

God is not against nice things, but He is against idols. He is not against increase, but He is against arrogance.

You can live in a nice house and still walk in humility.
You can drive a nice car and still carry a generous heart.

But if your identity is in the stuff, you've already lost the Kingdom purpose for your wealth.

Money Doesn't Define You, Mission Does
In the Kingdom, **wealth is a servant**, not a status. You're not valuable because you're rich. You're valuable because you're a child in the Kingdom.

When money becomes your identity, your sense of purpose rises and falls with your bank account. But when mission is your measure, you remain consistent in every season.

Some of the wealthiest people in God's eyes have little money, but massive impact. And some of the richest in this world are poor spiritually, because they're empty of purpose.

God Funds His Assignments
If God called you to it, He'll provide for it.
He is not short on strategy, partners, or supply.

When you walk in purpose, you can stop begging and start building. You can stop striving and start stewarding. The purpose of prosperity is not pleasure, it's participation. You are invited to partner with God in resourcing the earth with Heaven's agenda.

Declaration
I was not made for empty increase.
I am not chasing prosperity; I am fulfilling purpose.
My wealth is not for amusement, it's for assignment.
I carry power to get wealth so His covenant may be established.
I don't worship money, I wield it. I don't cling to blessing, I channel it.
I am trusted, I am assigned, and I am resourced to build for His glory.

Reflection Questions
1. How are you currently managing the resources God has given you?
2. Do you have a clear plan for budgeting, saving, giving, and growing?
3. Where have you seen the fruit of wise stewardship?
4. How does your stewardship reflect your faith and alignment with Heaven?

Chapter 7
The False Gospel of Greed

Confronting Counterfeit Prosperity

> *"Suppose someone thinks that godliness is a means to financial gain. From such withdraw yourself."*
>
> 1 Timothy 6:5 (paraphrased NKJV)

Not All Prosperity Is Kingdom

We must say this clearly: Not every message about money is a Kingdom message.

There is a version of prosperity preaching that exploits faith, manipulates the desperate, and uses Scripture to justify selfish ambition. This is not Kingdom. It's not just an error, it's a counterfeit gospel.

The true gospel never makes money the goal. It makes Jesus the King and wealth a servant.

When greed dresses up in religious language, it becomes a false gospel that sounds like truth, but leads to bondage, disillusionment, and idolatry.

This chapter is not written in anger, but in grief. Because many believers have been wounded, manipulated, or shamed in the name of *"seed faith," "financial favor,"* or *"prophetic offerings."*

It's time to tell the truth:
God is not a slot machine.
Money is not a measure of worth.

And faith is not a formula for luxury.

Signs of the False Gospel of Greed
The gospel of greed often sounds spiritual, but it reveals itself through patterns:
- Transactional language: *"If you sow $100, God will cancel your debt."*
- Celebrity culture: Elevating leaders based on income, image, and indulgence.
- Emotional coercion: Using fear or hype to pressure giving.
- Blessing for sale: Promising healing, breakthrough, or favor in exchange for a seed.
- Lavish lifestyles defended as faith: *"My Rolls Royce proves God is good."*

When giving becomes a bribe to get God's attention instead of a response to His goodness, the gospel has been hijacked.

God Is Not Manipulated by Money
The false prosperity gospel often preaches a transactional God:

"If you give this... God will do that."

But the true God is relational, not transactional. He doesn't respond to bribes. He responds to faith, obedience, and alignment.

He's not looking for people who give to get, He's looking for people who give because they've already received.

We don't give to make God move.
We give because He already has.

Paul Warned Us Clearly
Paul, writing to Timothy, warned of this exact distortion:

"Men of corrupt minds... who suppose that godliness is a means of gain. From such withdraw yourself." (1 Timothy 6:5)

In other words:
- If someone preaches that the purpose of godliness is personal gain, walk away.
- If someone uses ministry as a path to riches and indulgence, mark them.

Paul was not against prosperity. He taught generosity, giving, and sowing. But he was violently opposed to any system that used the gospel for greed.

Jesus Flipped the Tables

In Matthew 21, Jesus entered the temple and drove out the money changers.

Why? Because they had commercialized worship.
They turned sacred spaces into transaction zones.

And what did Jesus say?

"My house shall be called a house of prayer, but you have made it a den of thieves."

The false gospel of greed does the same today.
It turns God's house into a marketplace.
It packages promises in return for payments.
It cheapens the sacred and distorts the holy.

Jesus still flips tables.

How the Gospel of Greed Harms Believers

1. It sets false expectations. People give expecting wealth, and when it doesn't come, they feel betrayed.

2. It silences the poor. It suggests that poverty equals a lack of faith.
3. It idolizes wealth. It replaces the pursuit of holiness with the pursuit of materialism.
4. It burns bridges. Unbelievers see through it and reject not only the error, but the true gospel as well.
5. It breeds guilt and shame. People wonder, *"Did I not give enough?" "Is something wrong with my faith?"*

This is not what Jesus died for.

True Prosperity Glorifies the King
Here's how to tell the difference:

False Gospel of Greed	True Kingdom Prosperity
Self-centered	Christ-centered
Gives to get	Gives to glorify
Flaunts wealth	Stewards wealth
Proves worth by possessions	Reveals fruit by obedience
Uses scripture to get rich	Uses resources to fulfill assignment

Kingdom prosperity is never about accumulating for self, it's about impact, stewardship, and generational legacy.

It doesn't chase luxury, it pursues Lordship.

We Must Repent for Preaching Money Over the King
In some circles, the gospel has been reduced to a business pitch:
- *"Sow a seed into this anointing."*
- *"Your miracle is in your money."*
- *"God's about to make you a millionaire."*

KINGDOM WEALTH

But Jesus never said that.

He said:
- *"Deny yourself, take up your cross, and follow Me."*
- *"Seek first the Kingdom."*
- *"It's hard for the rich to enter the Kingdom, not because they're rich, but because they trust in it."*

We must repent for replacing the message of the Kingdom with the marketing of products.

We must return to Jesus, the true Treasure

You Can Be Blessed Without Bowing to Greed
Let's be clear: You can prosper without compromise.

You can:
- Live in increase without indulgence.
- Steward wealth without loving it.
- Walk in abundance without arrogance.

You can be fully blessed, fully obedient, and fully faithful.

God is not against you having things.
He's against those things having you.

Declaration
I reject the false gospel of greed.
I will not manipulate or be manipulated by money.
I live for the Kingdom, not for cash.
I am a giver, not a buyer of blessing.
I walk in prosperity with purity.
My life, my wealth, and my worship all belong to the Lord.

CHRISTOPHER TURNEY

I pursue purpose, not luxury.
And I honor the Giver above every gift.

Reflection Questions
1. What has your attitude toward tithing been, legalism, liberty, or something else?
2. Do you see giving as transactional or relational?
3. How does giving connect you to the house of God and the body of Christ?
4. What does it mean to discern the body in your giving?

"If we do not worship God, we will worship something else, and that something will shape our lives."

Tim Keller

Chapter 8
Wealth without Worship is Dangerous

Prosperity Must Never Outgrow Presence

> *"Beware that you do not forget the Lord your God... lest when you have eaten and are full... your heart is lifted up and you forget the Lord..."* Deuteronomy 8:11–14 (NKJV)

The Real Test of Wealth Is Not How Much You Gain, But Who You Become

Prosperity without intimacy with God is a setup for idolatry. When increase outpaces intimacy, you'll begin to worship the gift more than the Giver.

Wealth isn't neutral, it has weight. It reveals what's in your heart. It can serve the Kingdom, or it can seduce the soul.

This is why Scripture never condemns riches, but it always warns about them. Because wealth without worship is dangerous.

It feeds pride.
It fuels independence.
It creates a false sense of control.

You may not build a golden calf, but you'll still worship what you created.

The Pattern Is Ancient

When God brought Israel into the Promised Land, He gave them cities they didn't build, vineyards they didn't plant, and homes they didn't furnish.

But He warned them in Deuteronomy 8:

> *"When you have eaten and are full, and have built beautiful houses… when your herds and flocks multiply… your heart will be lifted up, and you will forget the Lord."*

In other words:

"Your danger is not in lack, it's in luxury."

God had no issue with their houses, their vineyards, or their wealth. His issue was when their wealth caused forgetfulness.

Worship is the remedy for forgetfulness.

Mammon and the Heart

Jesus said,

> *"You cannot serve God and Mammon."* (Matthew 6:24)

Mammon is not just money, it's a spirit that wants worship. It's a false god that promises security, status, and significance apart from God.

Mammon wants to take the place of dependency on the Father.
It whispers:
- *"You're in control now."*
- *"You don't need to pray—just pay."*
- *"You're powerful because you're rich."*

KINGDOM WEALTH

Mammon is a master. Jesus didn't say, *"You shouldn't serve God and Mammon"*, He said, "You cannot." Mammon's desire is to make you a servant to it. It wants to dictate where your money goes and to whom. If it can control your money, it can guide your heart.

It seeks to sanction your generosity, restrict your flow, and dominate your decision-making.

Mammon doesn't want to be managed; it wants to be obeyed. And its ultimate goal is to make you surrender stewardship and become its slave.

This is the same spirit that came to Jesus in the wilderness.

> *"Again, the devil took Him up on an exceedingly high mountain, and showed Him all the kingdoms of the world and their glory. And he said to Him, 'All these things I will give You if You will fall down and worship me.'"* Matthew 4:8–9 (NKJV)

The final temptation of Christ was not about food or fame, it was about worship for wealth. Satan offered Jesus the world, its systems, its glory, and its kingdoms, not through the cross, but through compromise. Not through obedience, but through flattery.

And the enemy still comes the same way to us, especially those who carry Kingdom DNA. He knows we are kings and priests unto our God (Revelation 1:6). He understands our regenerated nature, our authority, and our capacity to receive offerings and gifts.

So, he appeals to that royal identity, not to honor it, but to corrupt it.

Just like Jesus, we will be offered, not just tempted with lack, but flattered with abundance. Mammon will say, *"Look what I can give you. Look how much easier it would be if you served me."*

The danger isn't only in refusing to worship God. The danger is in accepting the offer of the subtle serpent, one who flatters, exalts, and offers everything…in exchange for your soul.

> *"For what will it profit a man if he gains the whole world, and loses his own soul?"*   Mark 8:36

Worship isn't just what you give to God. It's what you refuse to give to anything else.

But Kingdom prosperity doesn't sever trust, it deepens it.
It says:
- *"Everything I have is from God."*
- *"I will worship in increase the same way I did in lack."*
- *"Wealth is not my source, it's a resource."*

Worship Guards the Heart from Greed

The act of worship is not limited to song, it's the posture of dependence and devotion.
And when worship is genuine, it:
- Keeps you grateful in success
- Keeps you generous in abundance
- Keeps you humble in leadership
- Keeps you anchored in identity

Worship says, *"You gave it, Lord. You can take it. But my heart is Yours either way."*

Wealth can't steal your heart if it was never your treasure.

When Prosperity Leads to Pride

There's a temptation in prosperity to start believing your own success. You worked hard. You made wise moves. You built the business. You stewarded the opportunity.

And all of that may be true.

But it's also true that:

> "...What do you have that you did not receive? And if you received it, why do you boast as if you had not?" (1 Corinthians 4:7)

Prosperity can deceive you into self-reliance, making you think that you are the source of your success.

This is why God told Israel:

> "You shall remember the Lord your God, for it is He who gives you power to get wealth...". (Deut. 8:18)

If worship doesn't lead your wealth, wealth will mislead your worship.

True Worshipers Are Trusted with Wealth

Jesus said,

> "The Father is seeking those who will worship Him in spirit and in truth." (John 4:23)

God is not seeking fundraisers, He's seeking worshipers.

And worshipers can be trusted with abundance because they know what it's for.

Worshipers give quickly, obey freely, and steward wisely. They don't need wealth to worship, but if given wealth, they use it to glorify God.

Solomon Started in Worship... But Ended in Waste

Solomon began his reign by offering a thousand burnt offerings to the Lord. God visited him in a dream and gave him wisdom, wealth, and peace.

But later in life, Solomon's heart drifted. He began amassing gold, women, and foreign alliances. He multiplied horses, wealth, and wives, exactly what Deuteronomy 17 warned kings not to do.

And the Scripture says:

> *"His heart was not loyal to the Lord his God..."*   (1 Kings 11:4)

He didn't lose wealth. He lost worship.
And eventually, he lost legacy.

Solomon's story is a warning: **Worship must grow with wealth.**

Wealth Can Either Build Altars or Idols
- Abraham built altars wherever God prospered him.
- Solomon eventually built altars to false gods.

What you do with your wealth reveals who your heart belongs to. If your success silences your surrender, it wasn't Kingdom. If your increase eliminates intimacy, it wasn't worth it.

How to Keep Worship in the Center
1. Be generous and give as worship, not religious routine.
2. Build altars of thanksgiving every time God promotes or provides.
3. Stay in a community that values humility and presence over performance.
4. Engage in communion often to re-center your heart around Christ.

5. Ask the Lord regularly: "Is there anything You've blessed me with that's starting to compete with You?"

Declaration
I will not allow wealth to weaken my worship.
I remember the Lord, my God.
He gave me power to get wealth, and He alone is worthy of praise.
I tear down every idol and build altars of surrender.
I will never love money; I will love God and use money to serve His purposes.
I live in overflow, but I bow in reverence.
I worship with my hands, my heart, and my harvest.

Reflection Questions
1. What connection do you see between worship and your wallet?
2. Have you ever been tempted to worship God's gifts instead of God Himself?
3. How does Satan appeal to your royal identity in his temptations?
4. What would it look like to give as an act of worship in your current season?

Chapter 9
The Power to get Wealth

Understanding Deuteronomy 8:18
> *"But you shall remember the Lord your God, for it is He who gives you power to get wealth, that He may establish His covenant which He swore to your fathers, as it is this day."*
>
> Deuteronomy 8:18 (NKJV)

Wealth Is Not Given, It's Gained Through God-Given Power

God does not drop wealth into your lap.
He gives you power to get it. That one verse changes everything. Wealth in the Kingdom is not the result of favoritism, privilege, or even desperation, it flows from empowerment.

The Hebrew word for "power" is koach, meaning ability, strength, capacity, potential, or divine enablement.

This means:
- Wealth is not a lucky break.
- Wealth is not a reward for good behavior.
- Wealth is not automatic, even in the Kingdom.

It is the result of God's supernatural power working with your natural obedience.

You're not supposed to chase riches.

You're supposed to walk in the power to produce, create, generate, and increase, to get wealth.

Wealth Is Assignment-Driven
Deuteronomy 8:18 makes it clear:

"...that He may establish His covenant."

The power to get wealth is directly connected to **God's mission, not your materialism**.

He empowers you to generate wealth because:
- You are part of a covenant people
- He has Kingdom business to fulfill
- He needs resources to flow through righteous hands
- He wants His covenant to be seen, sustained, and spread

This means your business, investments, real estate, ministry, products, or career are not just jobs, they are vehicles for covenant fulfillment.

If you treat your profession as a paycheck only, you'll cap your increase. But if you treat it as a Kingdom pipeline, you'll position yourself for supernatural overflow.

Examples of the Power to Get Wealth in Scripture
1. **Joseph** — Interpreted Pharaoh's dream and was given power to steward Egypt's economy in famine (Genesis 41). His divine insight preserved nations and created storehouses of provision.

2. **Bezalel** — Anointed with wisdom and skill to create wealth for the tabernacle through craftsmanship (Exodus 31:1–5). Art and excellence became currency for worship.

3. **The Proverbs 31 Woman** — She considers a field and buys it, makes linen garments, and sells them. She is industrious, strategic, and profitable.

4. **Jesus' Parables** — The parable of the talents shows that God gives seed but expects multiplication (Matthew 25:14–30). Those who invest and steward receive more.

All these examples reveal one truth: God empowers people with creative capacity, wisdom, and favor to generate wealth, not for greed, but for Kingdom function.

Poverty is Powerlessness, Prosperity is Empowerment

Poverty tells you:
- You have no options.
- You are dependent on handouts.
- You are at the mercy of systems.

But the power to get wealth shifts your identity:
- You are a builder, not a beggar.
- You are a multiplier, not a mooch.
- You are a distributor, not a drainer.

When God gives you power, it will show up as:
- A divine idea
- A unique skill
- A sharp mind
- A bold strategy
- An open door
- An ability to create value

Your Wealth Is Hidden in Your Assignment

The power to get wealth **isn't generic, it's genetic**. It's not just customized to your calling; it's **coded into your Kingdom DNA**.

Generosity doesn't begin as a behavior; it begins as a birthright. The very word *"generosity"* comes from the root meaning *"of noble birth."* So, when you give, you're not just doing something kind, you're acting like who you truly are.

You were born again into **royalty**, and that means the capacity to release, fund, bless, build, and pour is already inside you. You don't just have power to get wealth, you carry the identity of one who distributes it freely.

Wealth, then, is not about excess, it's about expression.

It supplies the generous life with the means to manifest its nature.
Because you were born to give.
You were born to build.
You were born to overflow.

When God gives you power to get wealth, He's giving your identity room to operate.

This is why poverty feels suffocating to a son, it restricts the capacity to reflect the Father's nature.

Ask yourself:
- What part of my calling is waiting on the wealth I've been empowered to release?
- Where is my generosity being stifled by fear instead of fueled by identity?
- What would happen if I could actually stop limiting generosity to budget, and started tying it to birthright?

KINGDOM WEALTH

You are not simply a steward of wealth.
You are a son of generosity.
And your power to get wealth is proof that Heaven expects you to express the noble nature of the King.
As a son or daughter of God, you carry a built-in inheritance of fruitfulness, creativity, and dominion. It's not just what you're good at, it's who you are.

You were born again with capacity.
You were regenerated with resourcefulness.
And you've been entrusted with power on purpose.

For one, that power may manifest as innovation.
For another, hospitality.
For another, leadership, craftsmanship, strategy, or stewardship.
That means you don't have to compare yourself with others, you just need to discover what power is in your hands.

Ask yourself:
- What has God gifted me to do?
- What can I build that solves problems?
- What can I steward that multiplies?
- What flows easily when I'm walking in my lane?

You are not waiting for money.
You are waiting to recognize the power already in your possession.

Don't Just Pray for Wealth, Ask for Wisdom

Solomon didn't ask for riches.
He asked for wisdom, and riches came with it (1 Kings 3:9–13).

Why?

Because wisdom knows what to do with wealth.

And wisdom also knows how to create it.

If you're praying for financial breakthrough, don't just ask for a miracle, ask for a blueprint.
Ask for:
- Divine strategies
- Discipline
- Foresight
- Favor with the right people
- Courage to act
- Clarity to focus

Because God gives wealth through the gate of wisdom.

God Wants to Trust You With Power
Power is not given lightly.
With power comes responsibility.

And the Lord is looking for people who won't use His power for self-promotion, but for covenant advancement.

If God can trust you with power, He can trust you with provision.

The question is not *"Will God bless me?"*
It's *"Can I be trusted with what He gives?"*

Declaration
I have power to get wealth.
I am not chasing riches; I am walking in revelation.
I receive divine ideas, supernatural strategy, and Kingdom wisdom.
My wealth has a purpose, and my power has an assignment.
I will not fear success, I will steward it with humility.

KINGDOM WEALTH

I am positioned to produce, multiply, and release provision for Kingdom purposes.
I am trusted, empowered, and fruitful, in Jesus' name.

Reflection Questions
1. Do you believe you've been empowered to get wealth? Why or why not?
2. What unique gifts or callings has God given you that are tied to provision?
3. How does your identity affect your ability to release wealth?
4. What does generosity mean to you, and how does it express your noble birth?

Chapter 10
Grace-giving, the Prosperity of Sons

Giving from Identity, Not Obligation

"But as you abound in everything... see that you abound in this grace also."   2 Corinthians 8:7 (NKJV)

"God loves a cheerful giver."   2 Corinthians 9:7 (NKJV)

Grace-Giving Is the Highest Form of Prosperity

When it comes to wealth, we often think of receiving. But in the Kingdom, the truest mark of prosperity is the ability and willingness to give.

And not just give under pressure.
Not just give to get.
Not just give out of obligation.

Grace-giving is giving that flows from your nature, not your need. It is generous because it is grounded in identity.

Paul described giving as a "grace", not a duty, not a tax, not a transaction, but a divine capacity to release with joy.

Sons Give Because It's in Their Nature

True sons don't have to be manipulated into generosity. They give because they carry their Father's nature. God so loved the world that He gave, so we, made in His image, love and give as well.

Giving is not a religious ritual.

It's a relational response.

Sons give because generosity is their native language.

You can always tell an orphan spirit by how tightly someone clings to money. But you can always identify a son by how freely they release it.

Sons don't give to prove they're blessed.
Sons give because they know they're blessed.

Grace-Giving Breaks the Cycle of Manipulation
Sadly, many have been wounded by manipulative giving appeals:
- *"Sow this seed or miss your miracle."*
- *"Your breakthrough is tied to this offering."*
- *"God won't move until you release that amount."*

This turns giving into spiritual blackmail, and it produces either performance, guilt, or resentment. None of that reflects the Father's heart.

Grace-giving says: *"I give because I'm already loved, already blessed, and already seated in Christ."*

The Macedonian church in 2 Corinthians 8 gave out of poverty, with joy, and begged Paul for the opportunity to give.

Why?
Because grace was flowing, not guilt.

Tithing Was Lawful, But Grace-Giving Is Relational
Under the law, the tithe was required.
But in the Kingdom, grace doesn't abolish giving, it elevates it.

Grace doesn't lower the standard. It lifts the ceiling.

Jesus affirmed giving but called out those who gave without justice and mercy (Matthew 23:23).

Paul never made tithing a legal issue, but he constantly called the Church to generosity.

Tithing is a starting point. Grace-giving is a lifestyle. You don't give to unlock blessing; you give because the windows of Heaven are already open.

Sons don't measure generosity by percentages.
They measure it by obedience and joy.

Grace-Giving Is Always Purpose-Driven
Paul said in 2 Corinthians 9:

> *"God is able to make all grace abound toward you, that you, always having all sufficiency in all things, may have an abundance for every good work."*

Grace-giving is not random. It's not reckless.
It's strategic and Spirit-led.

You are resourced not just for survival, but for every good work.

That might include:
- Funding missions
- Supporting the local church
- Canceling someone's debt
- Starting a Kingdom business
- Building something that lasts beyond your lifetime

Grace-giving always has a target, Kingdom purpose.

Sons Give with Joy, Not Hesitation
Paul wrote:

> *"Let each one give as he purposes in his heart, not grudgingly or of necessity; for God loves a cheerful giver."* (2 Corinthians 9:7)

That word cheerful is hilaros in Greek, the root for hilarious. It means giving with delight, not duty.

Sons give like their Father, with gladness and generosity. They don't flinch when the Lord says, *"Release it."*
They live open-handed.
Because they know the Source never runs dry.

Generosity Is Royal Behavior
As mentioned in Chapter 9, the word *"generosity"* comes from Latin roots meaning *"of noble birth."* In other words: Generosity is not something you do **it's who you are**.

When you give, you're acting in alignment with your true identity.

You're not trying to be impressive; you're being authentic. Because nothing reflects the heart of the King more than a generous son.

The Prosperity of Sons Isn't What They Have, It's What They Release
There are wealthy people who hoard, and they're poor in spirit. There are modest believers who pour out, and they are rich in grace.

True prosperity isn't just accumulation.
It's activation, the flow of generosity, the joy of giving, the freedom of open hands.

KINGDOM WEALTH

The prosperity of sons is that they're never afraid to give, because they know they'll never run out.

Declaration
I am not an orphan, I am a son.
I do not give from guilt, I give from grace.
I am generous because it's in my DNA.
I will not be manipulated or pressured.
I give cheerfully, faithfully, and joyfully.
I give not to get, but because I've already received.
My Father is generous, and I reflect His nature.
My wealth is not measured by what I have, but by what I release.

Reflection Questions
1. How do you define grace-giving?
2. Where have you given out of compulsion instead of freedom?
3. How does your giving reflect your level of spiritual maturity?
4. What shifts when you give from identity rather than obligation?

Chapter 11
Stewardship, Managing what Heaven Trusts you With

Faithfulness Is the Pathway to Fruitfulness
> *"Moreover it is required in stewards that one be found faithful."*
> 1 Corinthians 4:2 (NKJV)

> *"Who then is the faithful and wise servant... whom his master made ruler over his household, to give them food in due season?"*
> Matthew 24:45

Increase Doesn't Come to the Entitled, It Comes to the Trusted

Wealth in the Kingdom is not merely about believing big or giving boldly. It's about managing wisely.

Faith will open the door.
Generosity will unlock the flow.
But stewardship determines what stays and multiplies.

God doesn't reward hype, He rewards handling. If you don't manage what you've been given, you disqualify yourself from what you're asking for.

That's why Jesus taught more parables about stewardship and money management than almost any other subject. He knew the issue was not about money, it was about trust.

You Don't Own It, You Oversee It

A steward is not an owner. A steward is one who manages what belongs to another.

In the Kingdom, everything belongs to the King, but He entrusts His resources to faithful sons and daughters who will manage them with integrity.

Psalm 24:1 says,

> *"The earth is the Lord's, and everything in it."*

That includes:
- Your money
- Your time
- Your talents
- Your platform
- Your opportunities
- Your relationships
- Your influence

You don't possess them, you steward them. And stewardship means you will give account for how you handled what Heaven placed in your hands.

Stewardship Starts Small

Jesus said,

> *"He who is faithful in what is least is faithful also in much."*
> (Luke 16:10)

Many believers pray for millions but mishandle hundreds. They ask for more, but don't master what they already have.

God isn't waiting to bless you; He's watching your handling.

Every breakthrough is preceded by a season of faithful stewardship.
- The man who multiplied talents was given more.
- The woman who poured oil in obedience saw it fill every vessel.
- The disciples who gathered fragments after feeding five thousand were learning divine efficiency, not waste.

You don't need more to start; you need to start with what's already in your hand.

Poor Stewardship Delays Divine Strategy

It's not always the devil blocking increase, sometimes it's disorder. Heaven won't pour out into a life that leaks.

God is not just a miracle worker, He's a wise investor. He puts resource into systems, plans, and people who won't squander it.

Ask yourself:
- Am I budgeting faithfully?
- Do I track what comes in and what goes out?
- Do I plan for giving, saving, building, and legacy?
- Am I open to counsel, strategy, and correction?

Prosperity with no stewardship is like pouring water into broken cisterns.

The prophet Haggai rebuked Israel, saying, *"You dwell in paneled houses, while the house of the Lord lies in ruins."* (Haggai 1:4)

Because their priorities were misaligned, God said it was like putting money into bags with holes in them. (Haggai 1:6)

That's the fruit of poor stewardship and misdirected resource, visible wealth with invisible loss. You can have income and still hemorrhage increase. You can earn more but keep less, because Heaven resists misalignment, even while loving you.

You Are Not Just a Receiver; You Are a Manager
Too many believers want to receive a harvest but are unprepared to handle it.

If God sent you double your income today, would you know what to do with it? Would you give strategically? Would you pay off debt or upgrade your lifestyle? Would you invest in your assignment, or spend out of impulse?

Stewardship doesn't start after the overflow. It prepares you for it.

You're not just called to receive resource, you're called to manage it with purpose, wisdom, and vision.

The Steward's Heart
A true Kingdom steward lives with these convictions:
1. Nothing I have belongs to me.
   It's all His.
2. Everything I have is meant to multiply.
   I am a fruitful branch, not a dead container.
3. I will not fear release.
   What flows from me will never bankrupt me.
4. I will not waste resource.
   I plan. I prepare. I plant. I protect.
5. I will always ask Heaven first.
   Stewardship begins with surrender.

Multiplication Comes Through Management

In Matthew 25, the parable of the talents reveals three stewards:
- One received five talents and doubled them.
- One received two and did the same.
- One buried the single talent in fear and was rebuked.

Jesus wasn't impressed with the amount. He rewarded the faithful managers and judged the fearful wasters.

Notice this:
The reward for good stewardship was more responsibility, not more relaxation.

"Well done... You were faithful over a few things, I will make you ruler over many." (Matt. 25:21)

Faithful stewardship doesn't just maintain, it multiplies.

Stewardship Is Worship

When you handle money with wisdom, you're not just being responsible, you're being reverent.

Every dollar you steward is a statement of honor to the God who gave it. When you plan, when you budget, when you build systems, you are saying, *"Lord, I value what You trust me with."*

That is worship.

Declaration
I am not an owner; I am a steward.
I manage what Heaven trusts me with.
I am faithful in little and prepared for more.
I will not waste, fear, or delay.

CHRISTOPHER TURNEY

I walk in wisdom, order, and strategy.
I am trustworthy, teachable, and prepared for increase.
I don't just receive wealth; I multiply it for Kingdom purpose.

Reflection Questions
1. What 'holes in your bag' might be hindering your increase?
2. Have you ever experienced loss due to mismanagement?
3. How are you planning not just to receive, but to retain and reproduce blessing?
4. What system of stewardship needs to be established or rebuilt in your life?

"Greed is not a financial issue. It's a heart issue."

Andy Stanley

Chapter 12
Sowing and Reaping in the Kingdom

Reclaiming the Law of Divine Return
> *"Do not be deceived, God is not mocked; for whatever a man sows, that he will also reap."*   Galatians 6:7 (NKJV)

> *"Give, and it will be given to you: good measure, pressed down, shaken together, and running over…"*   Luke 6:38 (NKJV)

Not a Formula, A Law
Sowing and reaping is not hype. It's not gimmick. It's a Kingdom law, rooted in creation, proven through covenant, and fulfilled in Christ.

It's not something you work to manipulate God, it's something you work in partnership with God.

God created the earth with seed-bearing potential. From Genesis onward, everything God created was designed to reproduce after its kind, seed, time, and harvest.

Sowing and reaping is not man's idea, it's God's divine system of multiplication, stewardship, and reward.

The Enemy Hijacked the Principle, Not the Power
Sadly, many have used the law of sowing and reaping to exploit people:
- *"Sow this exact amount for your miracle."*
- *"Your harvest is determined by the size of your seed."*

- *"Name your seed, and steadfastly claim your breakthrough."*

But just because men abused the principle doesn't mean we should abandon it. The enemy loves to counterfeit what works.

So, what we must do is reclaim the truth, not reject the law. Sowing and reaping is not about transactional manipulation, it's about covenant participation.

Sowing Is an Act of Faith and Partnership
When you sow in the Kingdom, you are saying:
- *"I trust God more than I trust my balance."*
- *"I believe in the soil of this assignment."*
- *"I'm investing in something eternal."*

Sowing is not just about money, it's about seed in every area:
- Time
- Words
- Service
- Relationships
- Resources
- Prayer
- Faith

Whatever you release, when sown in the Spirit, comes back multiplied.

Paul said:

> *"He who sows sparingly will also reap sparingly, and he who sows bountifully will also reap bountifully."* (2 Corinthians 9:6)

This is not pressure, it's promise.

You Sow Forward, Not Backward

Many people think sowing is repayment for what God did. But Kingdom sowing is always forward-facing, you're sowing into what's next, not what's past.

You don't pay God back. You sow into your next measure of fruitfulness. The farmer doesn't eat the seed, he plants it for the harvest.

The generous son doesn't cling to what he has, he releases it because he trusts the returning nature of God.

When you sow, you are activating a spiritual law that cannot fail:
- You don't just sow from overflow; you sow into overflow.
- You don't sow to prove something; you sow to partner with something.

Seed Must Be Sown in the Right Soil

Not all seed produces.

Even Jesus taught that seed must land in good ground (Matthew 13).

That means:
- Be Spirit-led in your giving.
- Sow into **assignment**, not just emotion.
- Sow where you're being fed, not just where you're being flattered.
- Sow into soil that aligns with your destiny.

The power of sowing is not in the number, it's in the obedience and alignment.

Sowing and Reaping Is a Process, Not a Magic Trick
Paul said:

> *"Let us not grow weary in well-doing, for in due season we shall reap if we do not lose heart."* (Galatians 6:9)

That tells us:
- There's a process
- There's a timing
- There's a temptation to quit
- There's a promise of return

Some seed comes back quickly.
Some comes back through time, obedience, and maturity.

But no Kingdom seed is ever wasted.

Even if man forgets, Heaven remembers.

You Can't Reap What You Don't Sow
Some pray for harvest but never plant. They declare overflow but hoard every opportunity. They beg God for breakthrough but never release what's in their hands.

Faith without sowing is fantasy.
You can't rebuke what you're called to release.

Even the widow in Zarephath received her miracle after she obeyed Elijah's word to bake the last cake.

> *"The bin of flour was not used up, nor did the jar of oil run dry…"* (1 Kings 17:16)

The seed she released unlocked the supply she needed.

God Gives Seed to the Sower
Paul said:

> *"Now may He who supplies seed to the sower, and bread for food, supply and multiply the seed you have sown..."*
>
> (2 Corinthians 9:10)

God doesn't just give money. He gives seed.

Seed is potential. It's instruction. It's opportunity. It's risk. It's vision. And God gives seed to the one who has a track record of sowing, not just asking.

If you want more seed, start sowing what you already have. God will multiply your capacity as you multiply your release.

Sowing Is Kingdom Warfare
Sowing breaks fear.
Sowing silences greed.
Sowing interrupts cycles of lack.
Sowing forces your flesh to bow to your spirit.

You declare war on Mammon every time you give generously in faith.

Sowing is how you tell the enemy:
"You don't rule me. My money isn't my master. My seed serves the King."

Declaration
I honor the law of sowing and reaping.
I do not give to get, I give to glorify.
I will not be manipulated, but I will be led by the Spirit.

CHRISTOPHER TURNEY

My seed is powerful, my heart is cheerful, and my soil is ready.
I release what I have because I trust the nature of my Father.
I sow forward, into purpose, into promise, and into legacy.
I will reap, because God cannot lie.

Reflection Questions
1. What is your current sowing pattern, and what is it producing?
2. Are you sowing where God has assigned you?
3. Do you expect a harvest, or have you stopped watching for increase?
4. How can you increase intentionality and faith in your sowing?

Chapter 13
Contentment and Increase, Friends, not Enemies

Gratitude in Every Season, Growth in Every Assignment

> *"Now godliness with contentment is great gain."*
> 1 Timothy 6:6 (NKJV)

> *"I have learned in whatever state I am, to be content."*
> Philippians 4:11 (NKJV)

You Can Be Grateful and Still Grow
Contentment is not complacency.
And increase is not greed.

In the Kingdom, contentment and increase walk hand-in-hand. You can live with full gratitude for what you have, while also stewarding your life to grow, multiply, and expand.

Contentment is about the posture of your heart.
Increase is about the movement of your purpose.

Paul wasn't poor when he said he learned to be content. He was empowered. He had been through seasons of both lack and abundance, and he learned to carry the same peace and purpose in both.

Contentment Is Not a Ceiling, It's a Foundation
Some teach contentment as a reason to stop dreaming. Others see increase as a sign they're discontent.

Both views are incomplete.

True contentment is not the absence of vision, it's the presence of peace. It means: *"I'm not striving. I'm not insecure. I'm not pressured. But I'm still pressing forward."*

Contentment says:
- I'm grateful for today.
- I trust God in every season.
- I don't need wealth to validate me.
- I'm blessed regardless of the balance.
- But I'm still called to steward and multiply.

The Spirit of Poverty Weaponizes Contentment

The poverty mindset takes the virtue of contentment and turns it into a spiritual excuse to settle.

It says:
- *"I don't need more"*, but what it really means is *"I'm afraid to want more."*
- *"I'm just content"*, but deep down it means *"I don't believe there's more for me."*
- *"I don't chase money"*, but underneath is *"I don't understand increase."*

Real contentment doesn't resist growth, it rests in God during growth. It doesn't cling to the past; it is anchored while moving into the future.

Increase Without Contentment Breeds Striving

On the other end of the spectrum, those who chase increase without contentment are never satisfied.

They:

- Always need more
- Attach their identity to income
- Measure success by applause or assets
- Feel like they're failing when they're not "flourishing" financially

This is not Kingdom prosperity, it's ambition in disguise. Increase must never become a replacement for inner peace. If more makes you anxious, you're not increasing, you're inflating. If blessing makes you prideful, you've gained goods but lost grounding.

God Wants You to Be Both Content and Fruitful
Jesus said:

> *"By this My Father is glorified, that you bear much fruit."*
> (John 15:8)

Fruitfulness is not opposed to contentment, it's the outworking of it.

When you are secure in who you are and who your Father is, you stop hustling for increase and start receiving it through alignment and stewardship.

You don't need more to feel valuable.
But because you are valuable, God entrusts you with more.

That's the tension, and the truth, of Kingdom living:

You are enough.
But there's more in you.
Be content.
But don't stop cultivating.

Contentment Prepares You to Handle Increase
Paul said:

"I have learned to be content..." (Philippians 4:11)

That word learned means trained over time.

You don't stumble into contentment.
You grow into it.
And the deeper your contentment, the more mature your increase will be.

Contentment says:
- *"I'm not shaken by gain or loss."*
- *"I'll tithe with $10 the same way I will with $10,000."*
- *"I'll live in peace whether I'm in a palace or a process."*
- *"God is my portion, the wealth He gives me is my assignment."*

Gratitude Grounds Generosity
The most generous people are not the wealthiest, they are the most content. Because when you're truly grateful, you release with joy, not fear.

Gratitude breaks the grip of greed.
It fuels the fire of generosity.
It keeps the hand open so Heaven can keep pouring.

When you are content in your soul, you'll be dangerous in your generosity, because the devil can't bribe, shame, or silence someone who knows they already have enough.

Contentment and Increase Are Not Competing, They're Completing

Think of **contentment as your roots**.
Think of **increase as your branches**.
The deeper your roots, the higher your branches can grow without falling. A life grounded in contentment will never be toppled by blessing.

And a life committed to growth will never be stagnant in peace.

God wants these in your life:
- **Stability** and **expansion**
- **Peace** and **progress**
- **Gratitude** and **growth**
- **Rest** and **release**

Declaration
I am content in Christ.
I am grateful for every season.
I am not striving, I'm stewarding.
I will not settle in false humility or spiritual fear.
I am both rooted and reaching.
I walk in peace, and I expect progress.
I rejoice today, and I prepare for tomorrow.
I am content, and I will increase.

Reflection Questions
1. Where have you confused contentment with complacency?
2. Are you resisting growth under the label of peace?
3. How has contentment protected you in past seasons?
4. What areas of increase do you feel God calling you into?

Chapter 14
Kingdom Economics, Heaven's System in the Earth

Living From God's Supply Chain

"Your kingdom come. Your will be done on earth as it is in heaven." N.   Matthew 6:10 (NKJV)

"For all these things the Gentiles seek. But your heavenly Father knows that you need all these things."   Matthew 6:32 (NKJV)

The Kingdom Has Its Own Economy

You were never meant to live by the world's system. When you entered the Kingdom, you were transferred into a new economy, one not governed by fear, inflation, manipulation, or scarcity.

God doesn't operate on Wall Street. He doesn't wait on global interest rates. He doesn't flinch at recessions.

The Kingdom runs on a different system, one ruled by righteousness, generosity, faith, and divine order.

This is what Jesus was teaching in Matthew 6:

"Don't worry like the Gentiles do. Your Father already knows what you need. Seek first the Kingdom, and all these things will be added to you."

This is the Kingdom economy:
- Seek first

- Sow faithfully
- Steward wisely
- Trust confidently
- Expect overflow, not because of effort, but because of alignment

The World Says: Save, Scrape, Survive

The Kingdom Says: Sow, Steward, Multiply

The world teaches you to hoard.
The Kingdom teaches you to flow.

The world says:
- Store it before you share it.
- Protect your portion.
- Get all you can and keep what you get.

But in the Kingdom, you gain by giving, and you receive by releasing.

God's economy is paradoxical:
- Give, and it shall be given to you.
- The generous soul will be made rich.
- He who refreshes others will himself be refreshed.

This is not mystical hype, it's a divine system.
It's not emotional, it's engineered by Heaven.

Heaven Responds to Honor and Obedience

The Kingdom economy doesn't run on manipulation or formulas. It runs on:
- Honor - placing value on God and His priorities.

- Obedience - responding to divine instruction, not human pressure.
- Faith - trusting that God's way produces God's results.
- Sowing - investing into Kingdom assignments and people.
- Stewardship - managing increase with integrity.

You can't buy favor, but you can live in a way that positions you for divine flow.

God's Supply Chain Is Supernatural
There is no shortage in Heaven.
There is no economic crisis in God's throne room.
There are no shipping delays in the Spirit.

When God wants to get resource to you, He doesn't check your credit score, He checks your heart, your faithfulness, and your alignment.

God may route provision through:
- A raven (Elijah)
- A fish (Peter)
- A widow (Zarephath)
- A wealthy partner (Lydia)
- A business breakthrough
- A dream, idea, or instruction

But make no mistake, He is the source, and He has a way to get it to you.

Kingdom Economics are Assignment-Driven
God fund's purpose, not popularity.
He backs obedience, not opportunism.

He releases provision in proportion to your assignment. That's why comparing your blessing with someone else's is pointless. If they're resourced more, it may be because they're responsible for more.

Prosperity in the Kingdom isn't based on equality of outcome, it's based on equality of faithfulness.

Jesus said in Luke 16:

> *"If you have not been faithful in the unrighteous mammon, who will commit to your trust the true riches?"*

The way you handle natural resources determines your access to spiritual authority.

Heaven Doesn't Respond to Need, It Responds to Faith

God is full of compassion but need alone doesn't move Heaven. Faith does.

The widow's mite moved Heaven. The Macedonian church's sacrificial giving moved Paul. The boy's lunch fed five thousand.

They didn't have the most, but they had faith in the system of Heaven.

God doesn't bless you based on pity. He blesses you based on participation.

Heaven's Flow Doesn't Skip Earth, It Moves Through It

Jesus taught us to pray:

> *"Your Kingdom come, Your will be done, on earth as it is in heaven."*

That includes provision.

KINGDOM WEALTH

God wants His economic order to invade this earth, through your hands.

You are the channel through which Heaven's economy flows:
- Into your family
- Into your church
- Into your city
- Into future generations

When you align with the Kingdom, you become a stream of blessing, not a reservoir, a distribution center, not a roadblock to the flow.

From Portion to the Whole: Living Beyond the Open Window

When many believers talk about God's blessings, they picture Malachi's "windows of heaven" pouring out a blessing until there's no more room to contain it. While this image is powerful, it is only a partial picture of what's available in the Kingdom. We were never meant to camp under an open window, we were meant to walk through an open door.

Jesus is that door. The moment you entered the Kingdom through Him, you stepped into a realm where all that the Father has is already yours. You are no longer positioned under a passing outpouring; you have been seated in a place of perpetual access.

The loaves and the fish are a perfect demonstration of this reality. In the natural, they were a fixed portion. Yet in the hands of the King, they multiplied without diminishing. Every person ate and was filled, and still there was more left over than what they started with. The Kingdom does not diminish. It does not run out. It does not ration.

When Isaiah prophesied of Messiah's rule, he declared:

> *"Of the increase of His government and peace there will be no end"*
> (Isaiah 9:7)

This means His reign is ever-expanding, His supply is ever-increasing.

Even in other areas of God's nature, this truth stands. When Jesus healed someone, He didn't say, "You've been given your portion of healing." He said, "Your faith has made you whole." The Kingdom does not operate on fractions; it deals in fullness.

The prodigal son's older brother lived with his father his whole life, yet still thought in portions: "You never gave me even a young goat." The father responded, "All I have is yours" (Luke 15:31). That's not a window; that's a vault. That's the whole estate.

We must shift from a portion mindset to a whole mindset. Portions imply limitation, whole implies unlimited access. This shift breaks comparison, because my receiving doesn't reduce your inheritance, and your increase doesn't shrink mine. In the Kingdom, the source is infinite, and every withdrawal leaves the account just as full as before.

You are not living on heaven's ration plan. You are living in the abundance of an unshakable Kingdom, where your position grants you the right to receive without fear of depleting the supply. The open window was an Old Covenant picture; the open door is a New Covenant reality.

Our Confession should be:
"I live from the whole, not the portion. I have walked through the door into the fullness of the Kingdom. My receiving does not

diminish the source, and my giving is a joyful overflow of God's unending supply".

We are not living under a window waiting for portions to be poured out, we have entered through the Door into the Kingdom.

In the Kingdom, you don't live by rations. You live by relationship. You don't receive from part of God's supply; you receive from the whole. And the whole is **never diminished**.

When Jesus multiplied the loaves and fishes, it wasn't a one-time miracle, it was a Kingdom demonstration. It showed that the **nature of the Kingdom** is **non-diminishing**. It does not run out. It does not shrink with use. It **multiplies when released**.

One person's blessing doesn't lessen the supply. In fact, Heaven's economy is the opposite, **it increases as it's given**. Isaiah said, *"Of the increase of His government and peace there will be no end"* (Isaiah 9:7). That means what flows from the throne never ceases, never lessens, and never fails.

When the prodigal's older brother heard of the feast, he was **angry about the portion**. But the father said, *"All I have is yours."* That's access, not allocation. That's inheritance, not allowance.

And when Jesus healed the woman with the issue of blood, He didn't say, "You've been helped." He said, *"Your faith has made you whole."* In the Kingdom, **wholeness** is the metric, not scraps, not leftovers, not even double portions. Sons receive the whole.

You are not living under the limited supply of a window. You are walking through The Door, Jesus Himself, into fullness, flow, and fruitfulness that never runs dry.

You Don't Live Under the Earthly Economy, You Live Under the Kingdom

You are in the world, but not of its systems.
You may have a job in the market, but your source is from above.

So, when inflation rises, you stay in peace.
When systems fail, you stay in faith.
When others panic, you position yourself to receive and release.

The Kingdom economy is unshakable.
And if you're aligned with the King, so are you.

Declaration
I live by Kingdom economics.
I don't operate in fear, I function in faith.
I'm not subject to the world's system, I'm aligned with Heaven's flow.
I honor, I sow, I steward, and I obey.
I expect provision, because I walk in assignment.
I'm not a reservoir, I'm a Kingdom distributor.
And I will never lack, because Heaven never runs out.

Reflection Questions
1. What worldly economic ideas have you unknowingly trusted?
2. How can you better align your finances with Kingdom priorities?
3. What step can you take to become a conduit of Heaven's flow?
4. Where have you seen God's supernatural supply chain in your life?

Chapter 15
Legacy Wealth, Leaving an Inheritance of Vision and Value

Because the Blessing Should Outlive You

"A good man leaves an inheritance to his children's children, but the wealth of the sinner is stored up for the righteous."
Proverbs 13:22 (NKJV)

"That the blessing of Abraham might come upon the Gentiles in Christ Jesus…" Galatians 3:14 (NKJV)

Prosperity Isn't Proven by Possession, It's Proven by Transfer

Kingdom wealth is never just about what you acquire, it's about what you impart.

Real wealth isn't measured by your bank account.
It's measured by what you pass on:
- Your values
- Your faith
- Your wisdom
- Your name
- Your discipline
- Your revelation
- Your favor
- Your spiritual and natural inheritance

The blessing of the Lord is designed to outlive you. Legacy wealth is proof that you understood you were blessed to be a blessing.

What You Leave Is More Powerful Than What You Earn

Jesus didn't leave property. He left a Kingdom. He didn't leave a business, He left an order, a Name, and an identity.

Paul left churches, sons, and doctrine.
Abraham left land, faith, and blessing.
Joseph left a prophetic word, and a nation preserved through famine.

The wealth that matters most isn't what you count, it's what you consecrate for the future.

We're Called to Build Generationally

God is the God of Abraham, Isaac, and Jacob.
He thinks in generations.

If your vision stops with you, it's too small.
If your wealth ends with you, it's incomplete.

Legacy doesn't mean extravagance, it means endurance. It means: "I stewarded today in a way that strengthens tomorrow."

Kingdom wealth is a torch, not a trophy.

Sons Inherit More Than Stuff

Legacy wealth includes money, but it's more than money.

Sons inherit:
- Instruction
- Culture
- Vision
- Responsibility
- Spiritual authority
- Favor
- The blueprint for how to walk in what you've walked in

Think about Elisha. He didn't ask for Elijah's income, he asked for his mantle. Real sons want more than things, they want assignment.

Fathers must raise sons who know how to:
- Honor the past without idolizing it
- Walk in inheritance without entitlement
- Expand the blessing without diluting the values

Don't Just Leave Resources, Leave Revelation

You may leave your children a home, but did you teach them how to make one?

You may leave them money, but did you teach them how to multiply and manage it?

You may leave them a name, but did you instill honor, identity, and integrity?

Revelation is the key to retaining wealth.
Without it, increase becomes a curse in the next generation.

That's why Moses constantly repeated:

"Teach these laws to your children... write them on your hearts... don't forget the Lord your God..."

Inheritance without revelation leads to rebellion.

The Wealth of the Wicked Is Not the Goal

Yes, Scripture says the wealth of the wicked is stored for the righteous. But that's not permission to envy the wicked or chase what they have.

It's a prophecy that God will transfer resources to those who are prepared to build something eternal.

If God gave you access to the wealth of nations, would your infrastructure be ready?
Would your values remain?
Would your purpose be clear?

Transfer without transformation is a missed opportunity.

You don't just want wealth, you want weight. Weight being the influence of your life:
- The weight of wisdom
- The weight of vision
- The weight of trust
- The weight of a Kingdom that never ends

Your Legacy Begins Today
You don't have to be a millionaire to build legacy wealth.

You can start by:
- Living generously
- Writing down vision
- Teaching your children how to give, sow, and invest
- Discipling sons and daughters in the faith
- Honoring your inheritance and building upon it
- Investing in missions, the Church, and future leaders

Legacy is not a someday concept.

It's a now decision, to live in a way that echoes in eternity.

Final Thoughts: The Blessing Outlives You
When your life is done, what will remain?
Will the Kingdom be stronger because you were here? Will your family, spiritual sons, church family and community be equipped to carry what you carried?

KINGDOM WEALTH

You were not blessed for a season; you were blessed for generations.

And because the blessing outlives you...

Live, give, sow, and build like the next generation depends on it.

Because it does.

Declaration
I am blessed to be a blessing.
I do not live for today; I live to leave a legacy.
I walk in wisdom, vision, and revelation.
I pass on more than wealth; I pass on values.
My children's children will rise with honor.
Sons and daughters will inherit spiritual authority and Kingdom order.
The blessing of the Lord on my life will not die with me, it will multiply through me.
I build for the future. I sow into eternity. I live for legacy.

Reflection Questions
1. What are you building that will outlive you?
2. Are you imparting vision and values along with provision?
3. How are you preparing your children, natural or spiritual, for inheritance?
4. What will your name, faith, and generosity say to future generations?

Chapter 16
The Inheritance of Sons: Wealth as a Birthright

> *"And if children, then heirs, heirs of God and joint heirs with Christ..."*   Romans 8:17 (NKJV)

When you entered the Kingdom, you didn't just gain salvation, you stepped into an inheritance. This inheritance is not wages for labor, but the birthright of a son or daughter of the King. In the world's system, you work for everything you get; in the Kingdom, you receive by virtue of identity.

Adam was placed in a finished work. He did not till the soil to make it produce; he stewarded the abundance that was already present. Likewise, as sons and daughters in Christ, we begin from fullness, not lack.

Wealth Is in the Bloodline

When you are born again, you are not simply adopted into God's family, you are regenerated with His DNA. That means Kingdom wealth is not something you have to "convince" God to give you; it's embedded in your spiritual genes.

In the natural, a child does not need to earn a place at the table. They don't need to negotiate for their father's provision. Access flows from relationship, not performance.

Inheritance vs. Wages
- Wages are based on hours, effort, and production.
- Inheritance is based on birth, relationship, and identity.

The world's mindset conditions us to strive for financial security. The Kingdom teaches us to steward what we've been entrusted with as heirs.

This is why an orphan spirit is so dangerous, it convinces you to fight for scraps when you've been given the whole table.

The Prodigal Son and the Elder Brother
In Luke 15, both sons lived beneath their inheritance:
- The younger son squandered it through waste.
- The older son served without joy, never realizing, "All I have is yours."

The Father didn't say, *"I will give you something."* He said, *"Everything that belongs to Me already belongs to you."*

This is a Kingdom wealth principle: God is not rationing out provision to you in fear of running out. His supply is unlimited, and your inheritance is secure.

Mephibosheth's Restoration
David's restoration of Saul's grandson Mephibosheth in 2 Samuel 9 is a picture of Kingdom inheritance. Though crippled, isolated, and without personal merit, Mephibosheth was brought to the king's table "as one of the king's sons."

That is how God restores us, not merely giving us "enough to get by," but seating us in a place of royal provision.

Living From the Table
As a son or daughter:
- You don't compete for resources; your provision is secure.
- You don't hoard in fear, your source is inexhaustible.
- You don't labor to earn; you steward what flows.

KINGDOM WEALTH

When you embrace your identity as an heir, wealth ceases to be a pursuit and becomes a position.

Declaration
I am an heir of God and a joint heir with Christ.
I live from inheritance, not wages.
The supply of Heaven is my source, and it does not run dry.
All that the Father has is mine, and I steward it with faith and joy.

Reflection Questions
1. How does the blueprint for Kingdom prosperity in this chapter differ from the world's model of wealth creation?
2. Which scripture in this chapter most strengthens your understanding of God's intent for Kingdom wealth?
3. In what ways does this chapter challenge the mindset of scarcity and replace it with God's abundance blueprint?
4. What is one action you can take this week to align your financial habits with the Kingdom prosperity principles outlined here?

Chapter 17
Generational Wealth and Kingdom Legacy

> *"A good man leaves an inheritance to his children's children."*
> Proverbs 13:22

Kingdom prosperity is never just about you. In God's design, wealth is meant to flow through you into the next generation, creating a legacy that outlives your lifetime.

In many families, each generation starts from scratch. The cycle repeats: one generation builds, the next consumes, and the third begins all over again. This is not the Kingdom pattern. The Kingdom calls us to break the cycle of starting over by building on what has already been established.

God Thinks in Generations
When God blessed Abraham, He made it clear the promise was for his descendants. When God called David, He established his throne for generations to come. God's blessing is never terminal; it's trans-generational.

Your stewardship today is not just about your comfort, it's about your children's future. When you handle increase with integrity now, you create momentum that the next generation can ride further than you could ever go on your own.

Wealth Is More Than Money
A true Kingdom inheritance is made of more than bank accounts or real estate. It includes:

- Values - The moral and spiritual compass that guides decisions.
- Vision - The clarity of purpose that keeps wealth aligned with Kingdom priorities.
- Virtue - The character that protects the blessing from becoming a curse.

Without these, financial inheritance becomes a liability instead of a blessing. This is why the transfer of wealth must be accompanied by the transfer of wisdom.

Training the Next Generation

Generational wealth is not automatic. It must be intentionally stewarded through teaching, modeling, and empowering the next generation to manage and multiply resources. This means:
- Involving them in giving decisions.
- Teaching them how to steward investments.
- Showing them how to recognize God as their ultimate source.

Your ceiling can become their floor if you are willing to prepare them.

The Down Payment Principle

God's blessing on you is not the end, it's a down payment for the generation after you. He trusts you to steward His resources not just for your lifetime, but for the Kingdom's ongoing work.

This is why it's essential to think in decades, not just days. Every decision you make now is a seed sown into the soil of the future.

The Kingdom Legacy Mindset

When you live with a generational mindset:
- You invest, not just spend.

KINGDOM WEALTH

- You plant trees you may never sit under.
- You make choices that your grandchildren will thank you for.

The world says, "Get all you can, while you can."
The Kingdom says, "Build something that outlives you."

Boom Factor:
God's blessing on you is a down payment for the generation after you.

Declaration
I am a generational thinker. I steward wealth as a trust from God, building a legacy of faith, values, and resources that will bless my children's children. I will not leave the next generation empty-handed, but fully equipped to advance the Kingdom further than I ever could.

Reflection Questions
1. **Long-Term Vision:**
   In what ways are you currently preparing financially and spiritually for the next generation?
2. **Wealth Beyond Money:**
   Which values, vision, or virtues do you most want to pass down to your children or spiritual heirs, and how are you actively instilling them?
3. **Breaking Cycles:**
   Are there generational cycles of lack or starting over in your family line that you need to break? What specific steps can you take to end them?
4. **The Down Payment Principle:**
   How does viewing God's blessing on your life as a "down payment" for the next generation shift your approach to stewardship today?

Chapter 18
The Currency of Honor

> *"He who receives a prophet in the name of a prophet shall receive a prophet's reward. And he who receives a righteous man in the name of a righteous man shall receive a righteous man's reward."*
> Matthew 10:41 (NKJV)

In the Kingdom, not all currency jingles in your pocket or appears on a balance sheet. There is a form of wealth invisible to the natural eye but undeniable in its impact, the currency of honor.

Honor in the Kingdom is not flattery. It is not mere politeness. It is the recognition and valuing of the God-given grace in a person, place, or assignment. When you honor correctly, you position yourself to receive from that grace.

Honor as a Seed

When you sow honor, you sow into a spiritual stream that can bring you provision, opportunity, and favor you could never engineer on your own. Jesus said that receiving a prophet in the name of a prophet positions you for a prophet's reward. That's not limited to spiritual insight, it includes tangible provision, strategic connections, and divine protection.

Honor is a seed that produces after its kind. Honor a teacher, you'll reap insight. Honor a giver, you'll reap generosity. Honor a builder, you'll reap resources and strategy for building.

How Honor Aligns You with Heaven's Flow

Honor is like an invisible pipeline. When you align yourself through honor, you connect directly to the flow of grace and resource on someone else's life.

Consider the Shunammite woman who honored Elisha by making a room for him. Her honor unlocked a prophetic word that broke barrenness in her life. Later, when famine struck, that same prophetic relationship preserved her household. Her story shows us that honor opens a stream you can draw from in times of both abundance and crisis.

How Dishonor Shuts Off the Flow

In Jesus' hometown, the people could not receive miracles, not because He lacked power, but because they lacked honor (Mark 6:4–6). They saw Him "after the flesh" and missed the grace He carried. Dishonor is like putting a kink in a hose, what could flow freely is suddenly restricted or stopped altogether.

Honor and Kingdom Wealth

We often think of wealth as the result of hard work, wisdom, or even divine blessing, and it is, but honor is one of the least recognized yet most powerful catalysts for prosperity.

David's covenant with Jonathan extended beyond Jonathan's lifetime. Because of honor, David sought out Mephibosheth and restored to him the wealth and land of his grandfather Saul.

Honor can reach into your future and pull resources you didn't even know had your name on them.

KINGDOM WEALTH

Boom Factor:
"Honor is the invisible wallet that Heaven fills."
When you honor, you're not losing dignity, you're making a deposit in an account only God can see, and only God can multiply."

Reflection Questions
1. How would you define "honor" in your own words, and how does it differ from flattery or politeness?
2. Who in your life has carried a grace or gift that you could access more fully through intentional honor?
3. What are some specific ways you can "make room" for the people, places, and assignments God has sent to bless you, as the Shunammite woman did for Elisha?
4. Have you ever experienced a moment when dishonor, your own or someone else's, blocked the flow of blessing? What did you learn from that experience?

Chapter 19
The Wealth of Nations

"The wealth of the Gentiles shall come to you." Isaiah 60:5 (NKJV)

"The silver is Mine, and the gold is Mine," says the Lord of hosts. Haggai 2:8 (NKJV)

God's Global Economy

When we talk about Kingdom wealth, we often think of personal provision, family stability, and ministry funding. But God's economy is not limited to your household or your city, it is global in scope. The Bible repeatedly points to a time when the resources of the nations will be drawn into the Kingdom for God's purposes.

Isaiah saw it: *"The wealth of the Gentiles shall come to you"* (Isaiah 60:5).

Haggai confirmed it: *"The silver is Mine, and the gold is Mine"* (Haggai 2:8).

This prophetic picture is not about greed. It's about alignment. God funds His global agenda with global resources. The "wealth of nations" is not a jackpot for personal indulgence; it is the resourcing of Heaven's plan for the earth.

Wealth Transfer: Purpose, Not Hype

There is a dangerous distortion in the modern church, a "wealth transfer" hype that paints a picture of believers waiting around for the riches of the world to drop into their laps without responsibility, stewardship, or alignment.

Biblical wealth transfer is purpose driven. Joseph didn't receive Egypt's wealth to build a palace for himself, he stewarded it to feed nations during famine. Solomon's wealth was not simply for luxury, it was to manifest wisdom that drew rulers and resources from around the globe.

If you want to be positioned for the wealth of nations, you must be:
- Faithful with what you have now - Wealth follows faithfulness, not entitlement.
- Rooted in Kingdom purpose - God funds assignments, not appetites.
- Prepared to steward on a global scale - Local faithfulness must scale to international responsibility.

The Principle of Attraction

The nations are drawn to light. Isaiah 60 begins not with wealth but with glory:
"Arise, shine; for your light has come! And the glory of the Lord is risen upon you... Nations shall come to your light, and kings to the brightness of your rising."

Wealth is attracted to vision, integrity, and divine favor. It is not first about the money, it is about the mantle. When the glory of the Lord rises on you, resources are magnetized toward the light of your assignment.

Practical Positioning for Global Resources
1. Think Beyond Local - Begin to see your calling in the context of nations, not just neighborhoods.
2. Build Integrity in Transactions - Nations will not invest in a dishonest steward.

3. Connect to Apostolic Networks - Global resourcing flows through Kingdom relationships.
4. Be Mission-Ready - When the opportunity comes, you must be ready to move, not still trying to get your affairs in order.

Prophetic Outlook

We are living in a time when God is shaking nations, politically, economically, and spiritually. Haggai 2 links the shaking of nations directly to the release of resources for His house. When systems collapse, people look for stability, and the Kingdom offers a foundation that cannot be shaken. In those moments, the wealth of the nations will seek a righteous steward.

"God funds His global agenda with global resources."

Reflection Questions
1. **Purpose over Possession** - How can you personally ensure that any increase you receive is directed toward God's Kingdom purpose rather than self-indulgence?
2. **Faithfulness Now** - In what specific areas can you demonstrate greater faithfulness with the resources you currently have so you are ready to steward greater wealth?
3. **Attracting Nations** - What "light" (vision, integrity, skill, or spiritual influence) has God placed in you that could attract resources from beyond your immediate environment?
4. **Global Perspective** - How does thinking beyond local needs to a global Kingdom mission shift the way you view and handle money?

Chapter 20
Kingdom Wealth and Apostolic Assignment

> *"Now the multitude of those who believed were of one heart and one soul; neither did anyone say that any of the things he possessed was his own, but they had all things in common. And with great power the apostles gave witness to the resurrection of the Lord Jesus. And great grace was upon them all."* Acts 4:32–33 (NKJV)

Prosperity With a Mission

Wealth in the Kingdom is never random, and it is never detached from purpose. Every time God places resources in the hands of His people, there is an assignment attached. Prosperity without a mission is like a wandering river, it may look powerful for a while, but without banks to guide it, it will eventually flood in the wrong direction.

In Acts 4, we see an apostolic model: provision was not hoarded but directed toward the expansion of the Kingdom and the meeting of needs among the saints. The result? Great grace was upon them all, and the testimony of Christ was amplified.

Provision Follows Purpose

God does not fund spiritual tourism; He funds spiritual transformation. Apostolic assignments carry a divine blueprint, and within that blueprint is a budget from Heaven. When you step fully into what God has called you to build, the necessary provision will be drawn to the vision.

Provision follows purpose like a shadow follows light. If you chase provision, you'll miss both. But if you pursue purpose, provision will always meet you along the way.

The Apostolic Edge
Apostolic work is not limited to planting churches, it's about establishing Kingdom government, culture, and influence in regions. This often requires large-scale resources:
- Facilities that function as Kingdom hubs.
- Funding for sending teams into unreached territories.
- Support for teaching, training, and equipping the saints.
- Resources for societal transformation projects.

Apostolic assignments demand apostolic-level provision. This is why God entrusts significant wealth to those who are proven to steward it for the sake of His Kingdom rather than their own empire.

From Local to Territorial Impact
When you view wealth through an apostolic lens, you stop thinking in terms of "my ministry" and start thinking in terms of "His Kingdom." Your financial decisions begin to shift:
- You invest in what has eternal impact.
- You measure success by transformation, not accumulation.
- You see yourself as a Kingdom distributor, not a personal stockpiler.

Your region's spiritual climate can change because of how you steward what God has placed in your hand.

Wealth With Assignment Is a Mighty Current
Money is neutral, it flows where it is directed. When directed by Kingdom vision, it becomes a mighty current that breaks through

barriers, fuels evangelism, rescues the oppressed, trains leaders, and establishes godly order in society.

When provision meets apostolic assignment, we see:
- Entire regions shifted toward righteousness.
- Generations equipped with truth.
- Communities transformed from dependency to destiny.

Boom factor: Wealth without mission is a wandering river, wealth with assignment is a mighty current.

Reflection Questions
1. In Acts 4, how did the early church demonstrate that provision was tied to Kingdom mission rather than personal gain?
2. How does understanding your personal Kingdom assignment influence the way you handle finances and resources?
3. What are some ways you can ensure that your wealth is directed toward eternal impact rather than temporary accumulation?
4. In your current season, what apostolic or Kingdom-building initiative might God be asking you to help fund or resource?

Chapter 21
The Inheritance of Sons and Daughters

Wealth as Birthright, Stewardship as Proof

"And if children, then heirs, heirs of God and joint heirs with Christ..."   Romans 8:17 (NKJV)

"Son, you are always with me, and all that I have is yours."   Luke 15:31 (NKJV)

"...that you may know... what are the riches of the glory of His inheritance in the saints."   Ephesians 1:18 (NKJV)

1) Inheritance: Not Wages, Identity

In the world, wealth is earned by hours, hustle, and hierarchy. In the Kingdom, wealth begins as inheritance, the fruit of who you are before it becomes the result of what you do. You don't negotiate for a seat at the table; you were born again into it.

- Wages measure effort.
- Inheritance reveals identity.
- Wages produce entitlement.
- Inheritance demands stewardship.

Kingdom prosperity starts with the revelation: "I am a child; therefore, I am an heir." But it never ends there; it matures into "I am a steward; therefore, I am trustworthy."

2) What We Inherit, and Who Inherits Us

Scripture speaks two ways about inheritance:

a) What we inherit in Christ
- Access to the Father (John 14:6)
- Authority to represent Him (Luke 10:19)
- Provision for assignment (Deut. 8:18)
- The Spirit as a down payment (Eph. 1:13–14)

b) We are His inheritance
Paul prays we'd know "the riches of the glory of His inheritance in the saints" (Eph. 1:18). You aren't only receiving an inheritance, you are one. God's favorite treasure isn't gold; it's people. That truth kills greed at the root. We steward things; we love people.

3) From Double Portion to "All I Have Is Yours"
The Old Covenant type was the firstborn's double portion (Deut. 21:17), a prophetic hint at fullness. In Christ, the shadow gives way to substance: the Father says, "All I have is yours." (Luke 15:31) The Kingdom doesn't ration; it entrusts. You're not clawing for a cut, you're learning to carry the whole with wisdom.

4) Heirs Under Guardians: Maturity Unlocks Management
Paul writes, "The heir, as long as he is a child, does not differ at all from a slave… but is under guardians and stewards until the time appointed by the father." (Gal. 4:1–2)

Translation: Inheritance is given at birth but governed by maturity. Heaven may hold back certain flows, not to punish, but to protect. Growth doesn't make you more of a son; it makes you a **safer steward.**

Signs you're graduating from "child" to "trusted":
- You plan generosity, not just feel it.
- You can delay gratification for legacy.

- You measure success by faithfulness, not applause.
- You build systems that multiply impact.

5) Taking Possession: The Joshua Pattern
Israel received land by promise but possessed it by process:
1. See it - Vision (Josh. 1:3).
2. Tread it - Action / presence on the ground.
3. Draw boundaries - Order, budgets, governance.
4. Dispossess giants - Break patterns, debts, and fears.
5. Cultivate - Turn land into storehouses, seed, and cities.

Kingdom inheritance isn't passive. Promise without process becomes presumption.

6) Enemies of Inheritance
- Esau's trade - Selling tomorrow for today's appetite (Gen. 25).
- The Orphan spirit - Hoarding from fear instead of stewarding from sonship.
- The Elder brother - Serving bitterly while standing outside of access (Luke 15).
- Squander & shame - The younger brother's waste followed by unworthiness (Luke 15:13–19).

The cure for all four is the Father's voice: "You are My child. Come to the table. All I have is yours, now learn to manage it."

7) Inheritance, Wealth, and Covenant
Deuteronomy 8:18 ties wealth to covenant: *"He gives you power to get wealth, that He may establish His covenant…"*

Wealth is not a trophy of self-importance; it's infrastructure for God's promise on the earth. Families, churches, cities, and nations are strengthened when heirs deploy inheritance toward covenant purposes.

8) Practical Framework: From Heirship to Handled

Spiritual:
- Daily confess identity: child → heir → steward.
- Practice worship-first giving to keep money a tool not a master.
- Stay planted in community; accountability protects inheritance.

Relational:
- Honor mentors and fathers/mothers, honor multiplies access.
- Train sons/daughters (natural & spiritual) in values and skills.

Financial:
- Create a Rule of Life: Give • Invest • Live.
- Institute governance: budgets, boards, advisors, audits.
- Estate planning: wills, trusts, beneficiary design, legacy letters.
- Build "storehouses": reserves that stabilize assignment through storms.

Operational:
- Systems for generosity (targets, timelines).
- Succession plans so the mission outlives the founder.
- Measure outcomes by transformation, not mere transactions.

9) Biblical Case Studies of Inheritance by Grace

- Mephibosheth (2 Sam. 9): from exile to the king's table, restored name, land, and seat.
- Zelophehad's daughters (Num. 27): inheritance secured by bold petition, a precedent for future generations.
- Abraham → Isaac → Jacob: promise carried through altars, obedience, and memory.

Each story reveals an heir who receives, then rightly orders, then releases inheritance for God's purposes.

Declaration
I am a son/daughter of the King.
I inherit by identity and prove it by stewardship.
I refuse Esau's trade, the orphan's fear, and the elder brother's bitterness.
I take possession through vision, order, and courage.
What I receive will bless generations.
All the Father has is mine, in Christ, and I will manage it for His glory.

Reflection Questions
1. **Identity Audit**: Where are you living like an employee instead of an heir? Name one belief to replace this week.
2. **Governance Step**: What system (budget, board, estate plan) must you put in place to handle increase? Act on it.
3. **Legacy Move**: Choose one value, one practice, and one story you will intentionally pass to the next generation this month.
4. **Possession Plan**: Identify one "territory" (market, ministry, neighborhood) you're called to tread, list the first three steps to begin.

About the Author

Apostle Christopher K. Turney is the founder and apostolic leader of Kingdom Reign Ministries, a global ministry dedicated to proclaiming and demonstrating the gospel of the Kingdom. With over four decades of ministry experience, he has traveled extensively, teaching, preaching, and equipping leaders, churches, and believers to walk in Kingdom authority, sonship, and purpose.

Known for his revelatory insight and ability to unfold Scripture with clarity and depth, Apostle Turney's message consistently calls the Church to return to Christ's original design: the manifestation of His Kingdom on earth. His teaching emphasizes the culture, government, and economy of the Kingdom, helping believers break free from religious tradition and embrace their full inheritance as sons and daughters of God.

In addition to Kingdom Wealth, Chris is the author of multiple books, including 'Called to Sonship', 'They Shall Be Saved', 'We Wrestle Not', 'Tithing: Law or Liberty', and 'Unashamed: From Shame to Sonship'. Each work carries his passion for grounding truth in the Word of God while calling readers to walk it out in everyday life.

Chris resides with his wife Jill, in the United States and continues to serve the Body of Christ through writing, teaching, and mentoring, raising up leaders who will carry the message of the Kingdom to the nations. He continues to travel and speak at conferences, seminars, and local churches.

For speaking invitations or ministry inquiries:
- Email: chris@krmchurch.com
- Mailing: 4550 NE Palmetto Dr.
  Jensen Beach, Florida 34957
- Web: www.chrisandjillturney.com

www.ingramcontent.com/pod-product-compliance
Lightning Source LLC
Chambersburg PA
CBHW072148160426
43197CB00012B/2291